Jesus and After

STUDIES IN EARLY CHRISTIANITY

Studies in Early Christianity

Jesus and After

The First Eighty Years

E Bruce Brooks

Warring States Project
University of Massachusetts at Amherst

2017

Jesus and After: The First Eighty Years
ISBN 978-1-936166-27-5 *cloth*, 67-1 *paper*, 87-9 *E-book*

Copyright © 2017 by E Bruce Brooks

LCCN 2017916508

The cover illustration is a detail from "Jesus Preaches in a Ship" by James Tissot (circa 1890), courtesy of the Brooklyn Museum.

PRINTED IN THE UNITED STATES OF AMERICA

To

Claude Goldsmid Montefiore

6 June 1858 – 9 July 1938

Preface

This book is not a History of Early Christianity. It rests on a careful philological analysis of the texts, and by highlights from those texts, it seeks to give a *sense* of that history by listening in on the early Jesus followers and their opponents. Those who followed Jesus' teachings during his lifetime and after, I call the Alpha Christians.

Later arose doctrines (the Resurrection and the Atonement) based on Jesus' death as *itself* having power to save. These ideas found a hearing among the Beta Christians; theirs is the Christianity of Paul. Alpha and Beta were hateful to each other, and both were hateful to Temple Judaism. This book introduces Alpha, then Beta, then watches as that three-way opposition plays itself out. Only brief space is given to a more individual or Gnostic variant, where people are saved by gaining knowledge of their own divine origin; it might be called Gamma Christianity.

These texts are often read as having the same message, as though they all came from the same moment in time. This book looks instead for the history connecting them, the evolution and sometimes the conflict of ideas that link one text to another, and ultimately to ourselves, in the present century. There is also history *within* some of the texts, as later material was added to keep that text current with the latest thinking about Jesus. That is where the philological analysis comes in: to identify those additions. This is not especially difficult. Here is Jesus in Mark, predicting that his followers will soon abandon him:

> Mark 14:27. And Jesus saith unto them, All ye shall fall away, for it is written, I will smite the shepherd, and the sheep shall be scattered abroad.
>
> [28] *Howbeit, after I am raised up, I will go before you into Galilee.*
>
> [29] But Peter said unto him, Although all shall fall away, yet will not I.

Peter looks right past the encouraging reassurance of verse 28, and responds instead to the challenge in verse 27. Then when Mark 14:29 was first written, Mark 14:28 *was not yet there*. This is how we recognize interpolations. And this interpolation is part of how we know that the doctrine of the Resurrection was not originally part of Mark's story of Jesus. In this way, it is possible to put the growth texts back to their original state. But identifying interpolations arouses opposition, and progress has thus been slow. Picking up on some results of previous scholarship, I have tried to continue that task for the texts here included (see further the footnotes and the list of Works Cited, page 185). For a text in both its original and its expanded form, see Chapters 52 and 53.

This book takes a historical view. Its Jesus is a human Jesus. He makes mistakes. His later followers also make mistakes. The Temple priests, turning away from what was widest in their own tradition, make their mistakes too. Some have found it helpful, and even liberating (not every churchgoer is comfortable with some Church doctrines) to have these changes traced out.

This book is for them.

Each chapter centers on a passage from the Bible or the related literature; it has an introduction (to identify the text, when it may not be widely familiar) and concluding Reflections. Readers are welcome to do their own reflecting; the book might provide material for an informal discussion group.

No apology for the Chinese characters which appear on a couple of pages. These people lived in a much wider world than we are accustomed to imagine.

My sense of the Gospels is that Mark was begun soon after Jesus' death, and updated well into the Forties. Matthew and Luke appeared in the Sixties, after the deaths of the leading Apostles. John came last of all, in the Eighties. The Gospels thus reflect three generations in the early history of Christianity. For these and other texts and events, see the Chronology on page 183.

What we call "texts" were more intensely regarded in ancient times. They were persuasions, as when someone is telling people what to do, in a sermon or an exposition. Or they were affirmations, as when people repeat something they already believe, and thereby strengthen themselves in that belief. The prayer Maranatha (Aramaic for "Come, Lord") is a wish that the Last Day should come *now*. When a singer finishes a hymn, and the hearers respond with "Hallelujah" ("Praise Jehovah") they are uniting with what has just been sung. I have tried to preserve something of that immediacy in these pages.

I have used the grammatically accurate American Standard Version (ASV), adjusting it where its archaism may mislead. One of its virtues is that it retains the historical present verbs which add so much vividness to Mark's story.

Readers with a Jewish perspective will note, perhaps with sadness, that with just a few differences in the direction it took, the Jesus movement might have remained what it was when it began: a Jewish sect. But a *universal* Jewish sect, attracting adherents from without as well as within the parent religion.

———·····———

Some early readers, those with missionary experience, have noted a certain missionary quality in this book. The book more or less wrote itself when I wasn't looking, but yeah, I suppose so. It goes beyond noting what happened, and prefers some things to others. It points out a very early form of belief which did not remain dominant, but may have its appeal for some today.

Claude G Montefiore, the most interesting of Jewish commentators on the Christian texts, did somewhat the same thing. His idea of Liberal Judaism included some preferences that readers of this book will recognize. Our views of the mistakes of Christianity and Judaism are not identical, but they run in similar directions, and I have thus felt it right to recognize him as a precursor. This book is dedicated to him.

E Bruce Brooks

Contents

Continued on Next Page

Alpha

1. The Promise to David
2 Samuel 7:8-17, 27-29

David was not the first King of Israel; that was Saul. He was not the most renowned; that was David's son, Solomon. David himself was known to later ages as a precocious warrior, a chivalrous opponent, and a singer of Psalms. From later ages comes this Promise of God to David, dictated to Nathan and relayed by him, and then the response of David, as he becomes a King, accepting the promise and sealing the covenant with God. God is speaking:

Now therefore thus shalt thou say unto my servant David, "Thus saith Jehovah of hosts. I took thee from the sheepcote, from following the sheep, that thou shouldest be prince over my people, over Israel; and I have been with thee whithersoever thou wentest, and have cut off all thine enemies from before thee; and I will make thee a great name, like unto the name of the great ones that are in the earth. And I will appoint a place for my people Israel, and will plant them, that they may dwell in their own place, and be moved no more, neither shall the children of wickedness afflict them any more, as at the first, and as from the day that I commanded judges to be over my people Israel, and I will cause thee to rest from all thine enemies. Moreover Jehovah telleth thee that Jehovah will make thee a house."

"When thy days are fulfilled, and thou shalt sleep with thy fathers, I will set up thy seed after thee, that shall proceed out of thy bowels, and I will establish his kingdom. He shall build a house for my name, and I will establish the throne of his kingdom for ever. I will be his father, and he shall be my son; if he commit iniquity, I will chasten him with the rod of men, and with the stripes of the children of men, but my lovingkindness shall not depart from him, as I took it from Saul, whom I put away before thee. And thy house and thy kingdom shall be made sure for ever before thee; thy throne shall be established for ever." According to all these words, and according to all this vision, so did Nathan speak unto David . . .

[David prays to God]: "For thou, O Jehovah of hosts, the God of Israel, hast revealed to thy servant, saying, I will build thee a house, therefore hath thy servant found in his heart to pray this prayer unto thee. And now, O Lord Jehovah, thou art God, and thy words are truth, and thou hast promised this good thing unto thy servant; now therefore let it please thee to bless the house of thy servant, that it may continue for ever before thee, for thou, O Lord Jehovah, hast spoken it, and with thy blessing, let the house of thy servant be blessed for ever."

———••••••———

Reflections

Thus was the covenant made. In later times, the line of David in fact ceased to rule, and Israel went into exile. But the promise of God was not forgotten. Israel sought to answer the riddle of why God had departed from it, and assured itself that if only things could be made right between God and Israel, God would return, and keep his promise. A later prophet, Malachi, added this detail, this further promise, for a waiting Israel:

> Behold, I send my messenger, and he shall prepare the way before me, and the Lord whom ye seek, will suddenly come to his Temple; and the messenger of the covenant, whom ye desire, behold, he cometh, saith Jehovah of Hosts. (Malachi 3:1)

That Jehovah, when he did return to Israel, would appear in the Temple, was only natural; the Temple was the proper abode of God, and it was there that sacrifices were unceasingly offered to him.

And so Israel awaited the appearance of the Lord of Hosts –

> Thus saith the Lord, Jehovah of Hosts, O my people that dwellest in Zion, be not afraid of the Assyrian, though he smite thee with the rod, and lift up his staff against thee, after the manner of Egypt. For yet a very little while, and the indignation shall be accomplished, and mine anger to his destruction . . . And it shall come to pass in that day that the burden shall depart from thy shoulder . . . (Isaiah 10:24-27)

> Of the increase of his government and of peace there shall be no end, upon the throne of David, and upon his Kingdom, to establish it, and to uphold it with justice and with righteousness from henceforth even for ever. (Isaiah 9:7)

Jehovah's hosts will drive out the Romans, and make Israel under the Messiah, as it had been once before under David, a great nation again.

Who would that Messiah be?

2. The Coming of John
Luke 1:65-79

John, the son of a Temple priest, was schooled in the cult of priestly purity. For him, the condition for Israel's return to God's favor was full observance of those prescriptions. When John appeared, he called for repentance, and many came to be baptized by him. Is John then the saviour of Israel? Precisely this had been prophesied of him, at his birth. The later writer Luke, who was seemingly close to the Baptist group, repeats that prophecy in this way:

And fear came on all that dwelt round about them, and all these sayings were noised abroad through all the hill country of Judaea. And all that heard them laid them up in their heart, saying, What then shall this child be? For the hand of the Lord was with him. And his father Zacharias was filled with the Holy Spirit, and prophesied, saying,

Blessed be the Lord, the God of Israel;
for he hath visited and wrought redemption for his people,
And raised up a horn of salvation for us,
in the house of his servant David.
As he spake by the mouth of his holy prophets
that have been from of old,
Salvation from our enemies,
and from the hand of all that hate us.
To show mercy toward our fathers,
and to remember his holy covenant.
The oath which he sware unto Abraham our father,
to grant unto us that we being delivered out of the hand of our enemies
Should serve him without fear,
in holiness and righteousness before him all our days.
Yea, and thou, child, shalt be called the prophet of the Most High,
for thou shalt go before the face of the Lord to make ready his ways;
To give knowledge of salvation unto his people
in the remission of their sins.
Because of the tender mercy of our God,
whereby the dayspring from on high shall visit us,
To shine upon them that sit in darkness and the shadow of death,
to guide our feet into the way of peace.

Reflections

Here, surely, is the Messiah long awaited. In ritual terms, John was the purest of the pure. His food and clothing were gathered straight from nature:

And John was clothed with camel's hair, and a leathern girdle about his loins, and did eat locusts and wild honey. (Mark 1:6)

Boldly did John preach against the defilement of the Roman presence, including the wrongs of their puppet ruler Herod, who had put away one wife and married another; a most conspicuous sin. And Herod, hearing of this, arrested John and put him to death.

The death of John was explained by his sect as due, not to any indiscretion, but to feminine intrigue. Mark's account, an early interpolation and the most sensationalistic thing in his Gospel, may well have come from the John sect. John Mark of Jerusalem was well placed to have observed John at first hand and to be in touch with his followers. Here, then, is how the John sect had probably told the story of John's death – in such a way as to exculpate John. Herod has heard of the miraculous deeds of Jesus, and reacts in this way:

But Herod, when he heard thereof, said, John whom I beheaded, he is risen. For Herod himself had sent forth and laid hold upon John, and bound him in prison for the sake of Herodias, his brother Philip's wife; for he had married her. For John said unto Herod, It is not lawful for thee to have thy brother's wife. And Herodias set herself against him, and desired to kill him; and she could not; for Herod feared John, knowing that he was a righteous and holy man, and kept him safe. And when he heard him, he was much perplexed, and he heard him gladly. And when a convenient day was come, that Herod on his birthday made a supper to his lords, and the high captains, and the chief men of Galilee; and when the daughter of Herodias herself came in and danced, she pleased Herod and them that sat at meat with him; and the king said unto the damsel, Ask of me whatsoever thou wilt, and I will give it thee. And he sware unto her, Whatsoever thou shalt ask of me, I will give it thee, unto the half of my kingdom. And she went out and said unto her mother, What shall I ask? And she said, The head of John the Baptizer . . . And the king was exceeding sorry, but for the sake of his oaths, and of them that sat at meat, he would not reject her. And straightway the king sent forth a soldier of his guard, and commanded to bring his head; and he went and beheaded him in the prison, and brought his head on a platter, and gave it to the damsel; and the damsel gave it to her mother.

And when his disciples heard thereof, they came and took up his corpse, and laid it in a tomb. (Mark 6:16-29)

The role which John had sought to fill, as the heir of God's promise to David, was now open for another candidate. In the light of John's failure, that candidate would have to rethink the whole proposition. What did God want? What was available in Scripture to guide the movement?

3. The Duty of Man
Numbers 31:7, Joshua 6:20-21, Micah 6:6-8

In the old view, God was tribal, and gave Israel victory in war:

And they warred against Midian, as Jehovah had commanded Moses, and they slew every male. (Numbers 31:7)

So the people shouted, and blew the trumpets; and it came to pass . . . that the wall fell down flat, so that the people went up into the city, every man straight before him, and they took the city. And they utterly destroyed all that was in the city, both man and woman, both old and young, and ox, and sheep, and ass, with the edge of the sword. (Joshua 6:20-21)

But time passed, and ideas changed. In the later Book of the Prophet Micah, after a passage in which God recounts all that he has accomplished for Israel, there suddenly occurs this passage, not spoken by God:

Wherewith shall I come before Jehovah,
and bow myself before the high God?
Shall I come before him with burnt offerings,
with calves a year old?
Will Jehovah be pleased with thousands of rams,
with ten thousand rivers of oil?
Shall I give my first-born for my transgression,
the fruit of my body for the sin of my soul?
He hath showed thee, O man, what is good,
and what doth Jehovah require of thee,
But to do justly, and to love kindness,
and to walk humbly with thy God? (Micah 6:6-8)

Reflections

This is one of three passages in the Scriptures where the sacrificial tradition is rejected in favor of an ethical idea of the duty of man. All are interpolations, and we do not know who wrote them, or when. Here are the other two:

> What unto me is the multitude of your sacrifices, saith Jehovah.
> I have had enough of the burnt-offerings of rams, and the fat of fed beasts,
>   and I delight not in the blood of bullocks, or of lambs, or of he-goats.
> When ye come to appear before me,
>   who hath required this at your hand, to trample my courts?
> Bring no more vain oblations: incense is an abomination unto me.
> New moon and Sabbath; the calling of assemblies –
>   I cannot away with iniquity and the solemn meeting
> Your new moons and your appointed feasts my soul hateth;
>   They are a trouble unto me; I am weary of bearing them.
> And when ye spread forth your hands, I will hide mine eyes from you;
>   Yea, when ye make many prayers, I will not hear:
>   your hands are full of blood.
> Wash you, make you clean,
>   put away the evil of your doings from you.
> Learn to do well:
>   seek justice, relieve the oppressed,
>   judge the fatherless, plead for the widow. (Isaiah 1:11-17)

And:

> I hate, I despise, your feasts,
> And I take no delight in your solemn assemblies.
> Yea, though ye offer me your burnt-offerings and meal-offerings,
> I will not accept them,
> Neither will I regard the peace-offerings of your fat beasts.
> Take thou away from me the noise of thy songs,
> For I will not hear the melody of thy viols.
> But let justice roll down as waters,
> And righteousness as a mighty stream. (Amos 5:21-24)

In the long war between the priestly and the human understanding of life, which has been fought out on many a continent and in many a sacred writing, here is one climactic Palestinian moment.

John's disciple Jesus, thinking on these prophecies, and on John's failure, will have understood why the sacrificial piety preached by John had been wrong, and why John himself had been executed. The whole basis was faulty. The ritual laws were not only beside the point, *they were not the point at all.* Something entirely different was needed.

The contribution of Jesus was to remember what that different thing was.

4. The Six Commandments
Mark 10:17-20a

Like John before him, Jesus preached "repentance and forgiveness." But with Jesus, the sins to be repented were far fewer, and the chance that people could be reconciled to God in this way was, accordingly, far greater. So was the chance that Israel as a whole could be reconciled to God, and that God in turn would give his favor again to Israel, and throw off the Roman occupation. From this fact came the dangers of which Jesus in Mark is constantly aware: his mission is directly anti-Roman.

What was the content of Jesus' version of the Law? That comes out in this story, which is from a later layer of Mark, but probably gives a correct account of this aspect of his teaching.

Judaism of the day had three requirements: devotion to God, obedience to his commandments, and charity toward others. Here is what Jesus taught about the second of these things: the commandments as he saw them.

In the story, a man asks what must be done to inherit eternal life. In answer, Jesus recites six Commandments, seemingly drawn from the usual Mosaic Ten, except that five are missing, and one against fraud has been added.

It has been the custom to read past this story, or to assume that in giving six commandments, Jesus means to imply the rest of the 613 commandments which experts identify in the Hebrew Bible. No, Jesus means his list to be complete. Here is the story.

And as he was going forth into the way, there ran one to him, and kneeled to him, and asked him, Teacher, what shall I do that I may inherit eternal life?

And Jesus said unto him, Why callest thou me good? None is good save one, even God. Thou knowest the commandments: Do not kill, Do not commit adultery, Do not steal, Do not bear false witness, Do not defraud, Honor thy father and mother.

And he said unto him, Teacher, all these things have I observed from my youth . . .

———————————··•··———————————

Reflections

We expect Jesus to recite the entire Decalogue. But he doesn't. Here is the Decalogue, from Deuteronomy 5:7-22. Items omitted by Jesus are bracketed:

> [Thou shalt have no other gods before me]
> [Thou shalt not make unto thee a graven image . . .]
> [Thou shalt not take the name of Jehovah thy god in vain . . .]
> [Observe the Sabbath Day, to keep it holy . . .]
> Honor thy father and thy mother . . .
> Thou shalt not kill
> Neither shalt thou commit adultery
> Neither shalt thou steal
> Neither shalt thou bear false witness against thy neighbor
> [Neither shalt thou covet thy neighbor's wife . . .]

As for fraud, that can be seen as a promotion from Deuteronomy 24:14-15:

> Thou shalt not oppress a hired servent that is poor and needy, whether he be of thy brethren or of thy sojourners that are in thy land within thy gates; in his day thou shalt give him his hire, neither shall the sun go down upon it (for he is poor, and setteth his heart upon it), lest he cry against thee unto Jehovah, and it be sin unto thee.

Students of Scripture will have seen that the early and later prophets conflict. How are such conflicts to be regarded? The view here taken by Jesus is that only the parts that do *not* conflict, that is, the overlap between the two, are valid for the present day. The later prophets, as the latest revelation of the will of God, have priority over the earlier prophets. The result is that the Mosaic commandments concerning God are omitted, and those concerning man are expanded. Merely *coveting* a neighbor's wife is not a sin; only the act of adultery would be a sin. There are thus no crimes of temptation or intention. Only acts are actionable. It is very simple.

To Jesus' hearers, this new system must have come as a relief and a release. The many rules of sacrificial piety, all of which were sins if broken, and the wages of any sin was death – what chance did one have? But to refrain from murder or theft, to be scrupulous with money owed – how hard is that, really? On that basis, pretty much anyone can enter into a state of sinlessness.

Jesus by no means broke with the political conception of Israel. He meant to realize the promise of God to David. But for that Davidic program, a majority of Israel must return to righteousness. What Jesus got from Micah was a *redefinition* of righteousness. On that new understanding, Israel can be saved. And if it can be saved, it can regain its sovereignty, and rule itself.

Jesus' view had its opponents. Not just in the Roman army of occupation, but also among the Jews.

5. The Traditions of the Fathers
Mark 7:1-23

Jesus did not regard the other Commandments as merely inessential, or think the Pharisaic elaborations of those Commandments merely superfluous. Jesus' critique went deeper. He found contradictions in the Rabbinic system. Here is his challenge to the Pharisees, the experts in the Law:

And there are gathered together unto him the Pharisees, and certain of the scribes who had come from Jerusalem, and had seen that some of his disciples ate their bread with defiled hands. And the Pharisees and the scribes ask him, Why walk not thy disciples according to the tradition of the elders, but eat their bread with defiled hands? And he said unto them, Well did Isaiah prophesy of you hypocrites, as it is written,

This people honoreth me with their lips,
but their heart is far from me.
But in vain they worship me,
teaching as doctrines the precepts of men.

Ye leave the commandment of God, and hold fast to the tradition of men.

And he said unto them, Full well do ye reject the commandment of God, that ye may keep your tradition. For Moses said, Honor thy father and mother; and He that speaketh evil of father or mother, let him die the death. But ye say, If a man shall say to his father or mother, That wherewith thou mightest have been profited by me is Qorban, that is to say, Given to God. Ye no longer suffer him to do aught for his father or his mother, making void the word of God by your tradition which ye have delivered. And many such like things ye do.

And he called to him the multitude again, and said unto them, Hear me all of you, and understand: There is nothing from without the man that going into him can defile him, but the things which proceed out of the man are those that defile the man. And when he was entered into the house from the multitude, his disciples asked of him the parable. And he saith unto them, Are ye so without understanding also? Perceive ye not, that whatsoever from without goeth into the man, it cannot defile him, because it goeth into his belly, and goeth out into the draught?

And he said, That which proceedeth out of the man, that defileth the man. For from within, out of the heart of men, evil thoughts proceed: fornications, thefts, murders, adulteries, covetings, wickednesses, deceit, lasciviousness, an evil eye, railing, pride, foolishness – all these things proceed from within, and defile the man.

Reflections

A parenthesis later added to the text by Mark explains, for readers not familiar with the system, that "defiled" hands are unwashed hands. Much is said in the Rabbinic texts about handwashing, and how much water is required for the hands to be considered clean. From the Mishnah tractate on Hands:

> A quarter-log of water do they pour for hands; for one, also for two. A half-log for three or four. A log for five and for ten and for a hundred. Rabbi Yose says, And on condition that for the last among them, there should not be less than a quarter-log. (Yadayim 1:1)

A log is a little over half a pint. The reason it is poured is that running water is regarded as clean, but standing water is liable to uncleanness.

The problem with Qorban, a vow of dedication to the Temple, is that when something is pledged to the Temple, it becomes forbidden for any personal use. This is one place where later rulings contradict the earlier ones, the ones proclaimed by Moses.

It is not a coincidence that the Rabbinic rulings not only describe the Temple sacrifices, and the purity rules applying to the priests who conduct the sacrifices, but specify tithes and offerings which directly benefit the Temple. These "dedications" are a legal dodge, a way of evading the duty to parents, and they are at the same time a device which benefits the Temple.

Mark has written the life of Jesus as one long conflict, not just with the Pharisees and their idea of Law, but also with the Temple, which sits at the center of the system and profits from it. Later on, it will be the Temple priests who locate a betrayer among Jesus' followers, arrest Jesus, and turn him over to the Romans to be executed.

As for what goes into the belly, and then goes out without defiling the person, this is perhaps the key to the whole position.[1] It is this which ethicizes the previous sacrificial piety rules, and casts the whole system of forbidden foods in a new light. It destroys that system, and replaces it with something to which anyone with inner ethical promptings can relate. Including the Gentiles, and it was in their interest that Mark, in final-editing his Gospel, not only translated the Aramaic sayings, but added explanatory notes like this one:

> This he said, making all foods clean. (Mark 7:19b)

The simplicity of this is astonishing. It reduces the quiddlings of the Pharisees to nothing. What does it leave in place, as the religious duty of the individual? What, for example, is the religious duty of a child?

---

[1] And not for the Jesus folk alone; it was there to be seen by any reader of Scripture. Montefiore 1/130 remarks that this is the line that was later taken by Liberal Judaism.

6. The Sins of the Children
Mark 9:42 and 10:13-14, 16

In Judaism, parents are responsible for their children, and any sins a child may commit are held against the parent. It is only on reaching adulthood that the child becomes personally responsible. The father, at his son's bar mitzvah, gives thanks that he is no longer liable for the transgressions of his son. The son indeed, having reached puberty, is capable of becoming a father himself, and of standing in the same relation of responsibility to his own children.

The view of Jesus was radically different, as these two passages suggest.

And whosoever shall cause one of these little ones that believe on me to stumble, it were better for him if a great millstone were hanged about his neck, and he were cast into the sea. (Mk 9:42)

And they were bringing unto him little children, that he should touch them, and the disciples rebuked them. But when Jesus saw it, he was moved with indignation, and said unto them, Suffer the little children to come unto me; forbid them not, for to such belongeth the Kingdom of God. And he took them in his arms, and blessed them, laying his hands on them. (Mk 10:13-14, 16)

Reflections

A widely accepted principle of law in antiquity is that one who is unaware of a law cannot be held responsible for breaking it. This is why lawcodes do not exist except in societies with a certain amount of popular literacy. A Jewish child will often spend some of the years of childhood studying the Jewish Law, against the time when knowledge of it will be assumed, and transgressions of it punished. In the view of Jesus, as suggested in these two passages, the child is not only capable of sin (though those who bring temptation to a child are liable to especially horrible punishments), and not only capable of entering the Kingdom, but is somehow *ideally prepared* to enter it: "For to such belongeth the Kingdom of God." Does this have anything to do with Jesus' opposition to the legal minutiae of the Pharisees, and his own adoption of a six-clause Law?[1]

The duty of man in Judaism consists in three things: acknowledgement of God as the only God, obedience to the Law of God, and alms, or charity toward the unfortunate. To a question about the greatest commandment, Jesus answers:

> The first is, Hear, O Israel, the Lord our God, the Lord is One. And thou shalt love the Lord thy God with all thy heart, and with all they soul, and with all thy mind, and with all thy strength. And the second is this: Thou shalt love thy neighbor as thyself. There is none other commandment greater than these. (Mk 12:29-31)

The first of these is the Shema; the second is from Leviticus 19:18. Montefiore says, "The bringing together of these two commandments is highly striking and suggestive. They are to this day the main part, though not the complete whole, of the Jewish religion." The rest of it is the Law. Jesus' six Commandments we have already seen; they are given at Mk 10:19. That is all. It can be written on one side of a 3×5 card, or if one has not command of writing, can be learned by rote in five minutes from someone else's 3×5 card. Erudition is not required.

Are there then child converts to the Jesus movement? Seemingly so. And they need remarkably little instruction to be fully cognizant of its requirements.

In some traditions, the child is not only human, but is the *ideal* human, the state which meditation of the Indian or Chinese variety seeks to recover; the state of infancy, which is also the state of utmost oneness with the cosmos. The meditation ideal or its equivalent can be seen to lie behind the Gnostic texts,[2] and possibly behind some of the more mystical passages in Paul.

Jesus belongs to an earlier, less cosmopolitan period. But in his own way, he shows a special feeling for the innocence and simplicity of childhood.

And in his healing, he also includes children.

---

[1] See Chapter 4.
[2] The best known of these is the Gospel of Thomas. We will meet it Chapter 62.

7. Jairus' Daughter
Mark 5:22-23, 35-43

Jesus in Mark is not just a partisan of a certain interpretation of Scripture, he is a teacher and healer in his own right. Mark gives frustratingly little detail about Jesus' teaching, other than to say that the crowds were impressed by it. But he does give several healing stories (many of which later got upgraded into miracle stories, but that is not our present subject). Probably the most touching of these is the healing of a child, the daughter of one Jairus. In our Bibles, this story is interrupted by another and later one. Here it is as Mark first wrote it, without that later interruption.

And there cometh one of the rulers of the synagogue, Jairus by name, and seeing him, he falleth at his feet, and beseecheth him much, saying, My little daughter is at the point of death, I pray thee that thou come and lay thy hands on her, that she may be made whole and live.

While he yet spake, they come from the ruler of the synagogue's house, saying, Thy daughter is dead; why troublest thou the Teacher any further? But Jesus, not heeding the word spoken, saith unto the ruler of the synagogue, Fear not, only believe. And he suffered no man to follow with him, save Peter, and Jacob, and John the brother of Jacob. And they come to the house of the ruler of the synagogue, and he beholdeth a tumult, and many weeping and wailing greatly. And when he was entered in, he saith unto them, Why make ye a tumult, and weep? The child is not dead, but sleepeth. And they laughed him to scorn.

But he, having put them all forth, taketh the father of the child and her mother, and them that were with him, and goeth in where the child was. And taking the child by the hand, he saith unto her, Talitha cumi.[1] And straightway the damsel rose up and walked, for she was twelve years old. And they were amazed straightway with a great amazement.

And he charged them much that no man should know this, and he commanded that something should be given her to eat.

---

[1]Mark later added a translation for non-speakers of Aramaic, "which is, being interpreted, "Damsel, I say unto thee, Arise." Mark gives Jesus' original Aramaic words at moments of special tension, including Jesus' last cry on the cross. Here, it is the word of command to the girl's spirit, which is efficacious only in its original language.

Reflections

Jesus chose five disciples (the Twelve are a later arrangement).[2] These were the brothers Peter and Andrew, shore fishermen; Jacob and John Zebedee, prosperous boat fishermen; and the tax collector Levi of Alphaeus. Levi seems to have stayed behind as manager in Capernaum. Andrew is scarcely heard of. The other three accompany Jesus as he heals and preaches. So also here.

Some have liked to see in this story an instance of Jesus raising the dead. But we should probably accept Jesus' diagnosis; he was there and we are not. What *was* his diagnosis? It was widely thought in antiquity that in sleep, or in a coma produced by illness, the person's soul leaves their body and goes off on its own. Some societies have elaborate procedures for calling back the soul; the classical Chinese texts preserve several of them. So when Jesus says she is merely in a coma and not dead, he means that she is still within the reach of a summoning formula. By telling her to rise, he is in effect recalling her soul.[3]

Luke is said to have been a physician. It is easy to show from his writings that, at any rate, he had a sense of medical terminology and medical procedure. In retelling the story of Jairus' daughter he corrects some of the medical details. Here is his version of the last part of Mark's story.

> But he, taking her by the hand, called, saying, Maiden, arise. And her spirit returned, and she rose up immediately, and he commanded that something be given her to eat. (Luke 8:54-55)

Jesus does not speak, *he calls*. Then, a detail not in Mark, *her spirit returned*. It may be doubted that Mark himself actually understood charismatic healing, though we may say with some confidence that Luke did.[4]

Jesus tells Jairus, "Fear not, only believe." Jairus is not the patient, but belief, whether of the patient or others involved, is part of the healing process. When that element is missing, not very much can be done.

Jairus knows that Jesus is a healer, one who heals by "laying on of hands." That is, Jesus has an established reputation as a healer. Why then does Jesus ask the parents not to mention the healing? Because accompanying all these healings is a message – the return of God to Israel – which is highly subversive, and Jesus does not want his whereabouts known to the Roman authorities.

The return of God to Israel required the *repentance* of Israel. This was Jesus' higher kind of healing: putting people right with God. Of necessity, he preached that politically dangerous message in a covert way.

---

[2]Eduard Meyer first noticed that the "Twelve" passages are exiguous in Mark.

[3]See the "Summoning the Soul" in the Chǔ Tsź anthology (Hawkes 101-109). Chinese ritual texts contain specific instructions for these summonings.

[4]For more of Luke's medical revisions of Mark, see Harnack **Luke the Physician**.

8. The Sermon by the Sea
Mark 4:3-32, minus later additions

Having pared the commandments down to their essentials, Jesus came to Galilee. He violated the Sabbath. He argued purity rules with the Pharisees. He associated with sinners, since that was where the work was: preaching to the already saved would not alter the proportion of the saved in Israel, and the whole point was that a majority of Israel should come to be obedient to God. Jesus therefore went among the unsaved.

But secretly. The program was anti-Roman, and so the message must be preached in veiled terms. Nor would Jesus do all the preaching; each must tell his neighbor, and he his neighbor. Only in that way could the message spread, not just in Galilee, but to diaspora Jews in the far ends of the Empire.

Jesus is here talking to his converts, who have been spreading the Word, but are discouraged at the slight results of their efforts. Not everyone believes. What does that mean? When does it go public? What will happen when it does?

Listen! A sower went out to sow. And as he sowed, some seed fell among the path, and the birds came and devoured it, Other seed fell on rocky ground, where it had not much soil, and straightway it sprang up, since it had no depth of soil, And when the sun rose, it was scorched, and since it had no root it withered away. Other seed fell among thorns, and the thorns grew up and choked it, and it yielded no grain. And other seeds fell into good soil and brought forth grain, growing up and increasing and yielding thirtyfold and sixtyfold and a hundredfold. And he said, He who has ears to hear, let him hear.

Is a lamp brought in to be put under a bushel, or under a bed, and not on a stand? For there is nothing hid, except to be made manifest, nor is anything secret, except to come to light. If any man has ears to hear, let him hear.

The kingdom of God is as if a man should scatter seed upon the ground, and should sleep and rise, night and day, and the seed should sprout and grow, he knows not how. The earth produces of itself, first the blade, then the ear, then the full grain in the ear. But when the grain is ripe, straightway he puts in the sickle, because the harvest has come.

With what can we compare the kingdom of God, or what parable shall we use for it? It is like a grain of mustard seed, which, when sown upon the ground, is the smallest of all the seeds on earth; Yet when it is sown it grows up and becomes the greatest of all shrubs, and puts forth large branches, so that the birds of the air can make nests in its shade.

---·..·..·---

Reflections

As Mark says, "*with many such parables* spake he the word unto them." That is, this is not a single-occasion sermon; it is a gathering of comparisons Jesus used to encourage his converts on many occasions. These were reported to Mark (himself a resident of Jerusalem) by someone at the Galilee end, and Mark has put them together. A second-century bishop, Papias of Hierapolis, criticized Mark for his lack of narrative order. That is quite right. This is why: Mark didn't have the details. And on this occasion, Mark probably found it effective to cluster some reported sayings together, to make a sermon.

Though indirectly expressed, the advice is easily decoded. To paraphrase:

Look what happens when you plant seed. Some is lost; some never bears fruit. Some of your preaching fails, some convert later turns cold. But the converts who are fruitful will more than make up for the others.

This thing is secret now; it has to be. But it will not always be secret. The whole point of this effort is to become manifest later on.

It has its own momentum; God is returning. Your effort is important, but whatever that result may be, when the time is ripe, God will appear.

When he does, our efforts will become a great blessing, giving shelter to many. The birds who have flown far will find a home again in Israel.

With this sort of encouragement, and with each telling others (we might call it contact missionarizing), the movement did spread far. It spread from house to house and from town to town. Within months it had reached the great cities: Alexandria in the south, Antioch in the north, Sinope up on the Black Sea, Ephesus on the Aegean, Philippi in Macedonia, Corinth in Achaia, Rome itself.

Wherever the named Apostles like Paul later went, these nameless sowers had brought the Word there before them. Alexandria was producing converts like Apollos, learned in Scripture (and since he was from an Alpha church, he had to be reinstructed in Beta by Paul's assistants).[1] Corinth had its "Christ" party, not associated with any named Apostle but only with the name of Jesus.[2] Those in Philippi had their hymn of Jesus ascending to Heaven. The seed had been planted in the Thirties, and by the Forties, when we begin to know of named Apostles, the plants were already growing all over the Mediterranean.

Not everyone was convinced, as the metaphor of the sower makes plain. More than that; some were alarmed.

---

[1] Acts 18:24-28; see Chapter 28. Apollos was fully converted to Paul's views, and later wrote the thoroughly Beta Epistle to the Hebrews.

[2] 1 Corinthians 1:12; see Chapter 32. The other parties at Corinth were those of Paul, Apollos, and Peter.

9. Friends and Family
Mark 3:19b-21 and 31-35

The spreading of the Word was slow enough that at least some converts needed to be encouraged. Not only that, but Jesus' friends and family thought that he was out of his mind. As well they might, since any anti-Roman program was likely to be suicidal.

We are back at Capernaum, in the house of Peter's mother-in-law, the headquarters of the movement. Jesus' local reputation is high. Crowds have come from far and near to hear him and be healed:

And he cometh into a house. And the multitude cometh together again, so that they could not so much as eat bread. And when his friends heard it, they went out to lay hold on him, for they said, He is beside himself.

And there come his mother and his brethren, and standing without, they sent unto him, calling him. And a multitude was sitting about him, and they say unto him, Behold, thy mother and thy brethren without seek for thee. And he answereth them and saith, Who is my mother and my brethren? And looking round on them that sat round about him, he saith, Behold my mother and my brethren! For whoseoever shall do the will of God, the same is my brother, and sister, and mother.

Reflections

Mark is a hard read, and this passage is notably offensive to the family feelings of its later readers. Luke and in his turn Matthew dutifully repeat it, though John, taking a firmer line, will recast it in a more family-friendly form.[1]

Meanwhile, not just this passage but throughout Mark, we learn that being a disciple of Jesus means a break with your previous life, including your family. Membership in the Jesus movement divides families, and it alienates friends. The point Mark is here making is that adherence to what Jesus has taught is more important than anything else.

Not only does membership in the Jesus movement divide one from one's friends and family, it will set one against the rest of the entire civilized world, including the power of Rome. Luke elaborates this in his Sermon on the Way; that Sermon we will meet presently. So yes, the value of being saved is infinite, but here is the cost.

Mark has been criticized for his historical presents: verbs in the present tense that refer to past actions. These are vulgar in English too, and translations tend to correct them. So do Matthew and Luke. Why does Mark do it? He does it for emphasis. It is his way of putting out a "red-letter Bible," with certain passages emphasized. Some of these emphasized passages are words of Jesus, and others are introductions to stories. The translation here used, the old American Standard Version, is the only one that systematically preserves these marks of emphasis. So the word "saith" ("says") should be taken as a highlight; a sign that Mark the story teller is leaning closer to us, across the table in the children's room of local library, one Friday morning, and looking straight at us, and using his voice to indicate to us: Here comes something really special.

"And he answereth them and saith, Who are my mother and my brethren?"

I don't know about you, but the other kids at the story table are wide-eyed with expectation: *Wow! What is Jesus going to say?*

What Jesus is going to say is, in a few words, the secret of living together as a new community. The secret is that *there is* a new community:

"Whosoever shall do the will of God, the same is my brother."

That much-needed community was not to be found among one's neighbors, not even the neighbors of Jesus, the people among whom he had grown up.

---

[1] See Chapter 51.

10. At Nazareth
Mark 6:1-6

Though he claimed to be realizing God's promise to David, Jesus himself acknowledges (in Mark 12:35-37) that he was not a descendant of David. Popular tradition later gave him a Davidic lineage (Matthew 1:1-16), and a birth in David's town, Bethlehem in Judaea. But early tradition says Nazareth in Galilee. Jesus was the son of a carpenter, Joseph, and his wife, Mary; he had several brothers and sisters. The boom town of Sepphoris was hours away. Joseph prospered. He could give Jesus and his next-born, Jacob, an education in the Scriptures. When Jesus began to preach, it was in Capernaum in Galilee, and not in any Judaean town. And he was successful, perhaps especially because of his gift for charismatic healing.

Then he returned to his home town, and that gift did not work as before.

And he went out from thence and he cometh into his own country, and his disciples follow him. And when the Sabbath was come, he began to teach in the synagogue, and many hearing him were astonished, saying, Whence hath this man these things? And, What is the wisdom that is given unto his man, and what mean such mighty works wrought by his hands? Is this not the carpenter, the son of Mary, and brother of Jacob, and Joses, and Judas, and Simon? And are not his sisters here with us? And they were offended in him.

And Jesus said, A prophet is not without honor, save in his own country, and among his own kin, and in his own house. And he could there do no mighty work, save that he laid his hands upon a few sick folk, and healed them. And he marveled at their unbelief.

And he went round about the villages teaching.

Reflections

This story, like the preceding one, is not a huge success for Jesus. Why then did Mark include it at all? The answer is simple: to show the divide between those who believe and those who do not, and to emphasize the newness of the community of the saved.

For the medically curious reader, along with the healing of Jairus' daughter, it shows how charismatic healing worked. The charismatic person, by touch or word, makes contact with the sick person, but the sick person must also contribute. What the sick one contributes is faith: confidence that the healer can heal. It is this two-way relation that makes possible the healings that can be done this way. Without the patient's unquestioning confidence in the process (and this applies to modern surgery also), there is less chance of success.

The point of Nazareth for some later writers was Jesus' rejection by the age. The point for Mark was the contrast between those who did and didn't believe. And that Jesus' own people, those who had known him from his childhood, were among those who didn't.

But at some point, encouraged by the enthusiasm of others, including reports from the distant places to which the Word had been carried, Jesus felt that Israel in sufficient numbers had turned to God. There was a critical mass. The time had thus come for God to return to his Temple.

But the Temple itself was not ready. The prophet Zechariah (and Jesus had studied these people carefully) looked forward to the day when

> There shall be no more a trader in the house of Jehovah of hosts on that day. (Zech 14:20-21, the last line of Zechariah)

And so Jesus and a picked group of his followers set out for the Temple, prepared to solve that one remaining problem. The Temple itself was fouled with the filth of commercial trade, and that had to be dealt with.

11. Approaching the Temple
Mark 11:1-17, omitting later material

When Elijah had ascended to Heaven at his death, his disciple Elisha had glimpsed God's chariots of fire (2 Kings 2:11 and 6:7). Many were now saved on the basis of the Six Commandments. It remained for God to return with his chariots of fire, and expel the occupying army. Except that the Temple itself, as Nehemiah 13:15-22 had warned, was defiled by the traders in its precincts. To solve this problem needed coordination between the Galilee party and their contacts in Jerusalem, meeting at Mark's mother's big house in Jerusalem.[1] Here is how the secret preparations, passwords and all, looked to young Mark.

And when they draw nigh unto Jerusalem, unto Bethphage and Bethany, at the Mount of Olives, he sendeth two of his disciples, and saith unto them, Go your way into the village that is over against you, and straightway as ye enter into it, ye shall find a colt tied, whereon no man ever sat; loose him and bring him. And if any one say unto you, Why do ye this, say ye, The Lord hath need of him, and straightway he will send him back hither. And they went away, and found a colt tied at the door without in the open street, and they loose him. And certain of them that stood there said unto them, What do ye, loosing the colt? and they said unto them even as Jesus had said, and they let them go, and they bring the colt unto Jesus, and cast on him their garments, and he sat upon him.[2]

And many spread their garments upon the way, and others branches which they had cut from the fields. And they that went before, and they that followed, cried, Hosanna, Blessed is the Kingdom that cometh, the Kingdom of our father David; Hosanna in the highest. And he entered into Jerusalem, into the Temple, and when he had looked round about upon all things, it being now eventide, he went out unto Bethany.

And on the morrow, when they were come out from Bethany, they come to Jerusalem, and he entered into the Temple, and began to cast out them that sold and them that bought in the Temple, and overthrew the tables of the money changers, and the seats of them that sold doves, and he would not suffer that any man should carry a vessel through the Temple. And he taught, and said unto them, Is it not written, My house shall be called a house of prayer for all nations?[3] But ye have made it a den of robbers.

---

[1] All these details we know from Mark's contemporary Luke; see Acts 12:12-17. The maid's name was Rhoda.

[2] This was an arranged fulfilment of the prophecy of Zechariah 9:9

[3] Isaiah 56:7. The image is repeated in God's accusation at Jeremiah 7:11.

Reflections

But nothing happened.

The party left the city for their lodging in Bethany. But it was the Passover, and there were covert arrangements for eating the Passover in the city:

> And on the first day of unleavened bread, when they sacrificed the Passover, his disciples say unto him, Where wilt thou that we go and make ready that thou mayest eat the Passover? And he sendeth two of his disciples and saith unto them, Go into the city, and there shall meet you a man bearing a pitcher of water; follow him, and wheresoever he shall enter in, say to the master of the house, Where is my guest-chamber, where I shall eat the Passover with my disciples? And he will show you a large upper room furnished and ready, and there make ready for us. And the disciples went forth and came into the city, and found as he had said unto them, and they made ready the Passover. (Mk 14:12-16)

Here are the signs and counter-signs; this is a covert operation.

So the party are now in Mark's mother's house, and no one knows it. Except that Judas, one of the party, has realized that the thing is a fizzle, and plans to get out while he can. He is in on the prearrangements, and has told the Temple police where Jesus will be – in the city, and thus within their reach. Presently Jesus and the others finish their meal, and depart:

> When they had sung a hymn,[4] they went out unto the Mount of Olives. (Mark 14:26)

The Temple police show up, but nobody is there. Judas, knowing where they are likely to be, leads the police detail there. Young Mark, roused from sleep, is alarmed. Throwing a sheet over himself, he runs ahead to warn them, but no sooner has Mark gotten there, than the police arrive, and after a brief scuffle, they arrest Jesus. His disciples get away. So does young Mark:

> And they all left him and fled. And a certain young man followed with them, having a linen cloth cast about him, over his naked body, and they lay hold on him, but he left the linen cloth, and fled naked.[5] (Mark 14:51-52)

Thus does Mark write himself into the story. And why not? He was there.

What happened next was foregone.

---

[4]The hymns proper to the Passover occasion, at least as celebrated by the priests, were the Hallel, Psalms 113-118. The last of these is especially appropriate to a time when God would come to save his people. Part of it goes:

> Jehovah is my strength and song,
> and he is become my salvation.
> The voice of rejoicing and salvation is in the tents of the righteous,
> the right hand of Jehovah doeth valiantly . . . (Psalm 118:14-15)

[5]An echo of Amos 2:16. Perhaps a justification for what might seem cowardice?

12. The Crucifixion
Mark 15:16-37

The Temple authorities held Jesus overnight, and next morning sent him to the Roman governor Pilate, who on the occasion of the festival, when some disturbance might be feared, was in town with a detachment of his soldiers. After a brief hearing, Pilate condemns Jesus as a would-be King of the Jews. The soldiers mock him, and then carry out the crucifixion, an agonizing form of death used for rebels and other offenders against the state.

Here is Mark's eyewitness report, with the names of other eyewitnesses.

And the soldiers led him away inside the palace. They call together the whole battalion and clothe him in a purple cloak; plaiting a crown of thorns they put it on him. They began to salute him, Hail, King of the Jews! And they struck his head with a reed, and spat upon him, and they knelt down in homage to him. And when they had mocked him, they stripped him of the purple cloak, and put his own clothes on him. And they lead him out to crucify him.

And they compel a passer-by, Simon of Cyrene, who was coming in from the country, the father of Alexander and Rufus, to carry his cross. And they bring him to the place called Golgotha. And they offered him wine mingled with myrrh, but he did not take it.

And they crucify him, and divide his garments among them, casting lots for them, to decide what each should take. And it was the third hour when they crucified him. The inscription of the charge against him read, King of the Jews. And with him they crucify two robbers, one on his right and one on his left. And those who passed by derided him, wagging their heads and saying, Aha! You who would destroy the temple and build it in three days, Save yourself, and come down from the cross! So also the chief priests mocked him to one another with the scribes, saying, He saved others, he cannot save himself. Let the Anointed, the King of Israel, come down now from the cross, that we may see and believe. Those who were crucified with him also reviled him. And when the sixth hour had come, there was darkness over the whole land until the ninth hour. And at the ninth hour, Jesus cried with a loud voice, Eloi, Eloi, lama sabachthani?[1] And some of the bystanders hearing it said, Behold, he is calling Elijah. And one ran and, filling a sponge full of vinegar, put it on a reed and gave it to him to drink, saying, Wait, let us see whether Elijah will come to take him down. And Jesus uttered a loud cry, and breathed his last.

------ ·· • ·· ------

[1]In Aramaic; the meaning is "My God, my God, why hast thou forsaken me?"

Reflections

Through the Crucifixion scene, Mark has scattered echoes of Psalm 22. Here is how the end of the scene reads, with those echoes emphasized:

> And they crucify him, and **divide his garments among them, casting lots for them, to decide what each should take**. And it was the third hour when they crucified him. The inscription of the charge against him read, King of the Jews. And with him they crucify two robbers, one on his right and one on his left. And those who passed by **derided him, wagging their heads and saying**, Aha! You who would destroy the temple and build it in three days, Save yourself, and come down from the cross! So also the chief priests mocked him to one another with the scribes, saying, He saved others, he cannot save himself. **Let the Anointed, the King of Israel, come down now from the cross,** that we may see and believe. Those who were crucified with him also reviled him. And when the sixth hour had come, there was darkness over the whole land until the ninth hour. And at the ninth hour, Jesus cried with a loud voice, **Eloi, Eloi, lama sabachthani?** And some of the bystanders hearing it said, Behold, he is calling Elijah. And one ran and, filling a sponge full of vinegar, put it on a reed and gave it to him to drink, saying, Wait, **let us see whether Elijah will come to take him down**. And Jesus uttered a loud cry, and breathed his last.

In the minds of Mark's devout hearers, Psalm 22 continues this way:

> Ye that fear Jehovah, praise him,
> All the seed of Jacob, glorify him.
> And stand in awe of him,
> All ye seed of Israel.
>
> For he hath not despised nor abhorred
> the affliction of the afflicted;
> Neither hath he hid his face from him.
> But when he cried unto him, he heard.

This implies that the seeming defeat of Jesus will after all end in a triumph. And that triumph is written into Mark, in the very last line of Mark's Gospel as he originally wrote it.

13. The Rending of the Veil
Mark 15:38

Mark has arranged his original account of Jesus as a long conflict between Jesus and the Pharisees. That story would seem to end with Jesus' death, and indeed, the Davidic Messiah program did end at that point. No one ever refers to it again (save to deny that Jesus intended any such thing). But Mark saves something by focusing instead on the question of the Law; the dispute with the Pharisees. For that conflict, Mark provides a positive ending. An unseen hand, acting from above and apparently that of God, rends the veil which protects the Holy of Holies from defilement, and, in effect, desacralizes the Temple itself. The Pharisee rules, based on the Temple purity cult, are abolished.

This is surely one of the most abrupt concluding scenes in all of literature. Jesus in the preceding verse "uttered a loud cry, and gave up the ghost." Then:

And the veil of the Temple was rent in two, from the top to the bottom.

Reflections

It is doubtful that this took place, but for readers or hearers familiar with the Temple, and envisioning the Jesus story as they go, it has tremendous impact. Mark had prepared everyone for a positive ending during the Crucifixion scene, with its background music from Psalm 22, whose unquoted ending, supplied by the memories of Mark's audience, spoke of vindication and not of defeat.

Now we have reached the end of the story; the background music is over. Suddenly we have this violent and unexpected event, showing just *what* victory has been salvaged from this seeming defeat.

The victory was over the quiddling rules of the Pharisees, the overgrowth of the Law, which Jesus had consistently opposed. His view is now validated, by God himself. Jesus' program, the Law reduced to its ethical essentials, is affirmed as valid. Obedience to it produces a condition of personal sinlessness. No longer as a component of the righteousness of Israel, that is not the issue, but as a guarantee of personal salvation. And with that hope and that assurance, the followers of Jesus went forward into the future.

Such was Mark's contribution. It was the first account, and also the first *interpretation*, of Jesus' life and death. Mark, located at the Jerusalem end of the Jesus movement (the other end had its center at Capernaum in Galilee), was the first theoretician of the Jesus movement. He interpreted it to itself. He saw it not as Judaism versus occupying Rome, disputing who should rule in Israel, but as Jesus versus Temple Judaism, over the meaning and extent of the Law.

Together with Peter's assurance that Jesus was still in being and would return at the Last Days, Mark's interpretation converted the hope of the Jesus movement from something grandly national to something intensely personal. Something that could, and did, survive the failed Messianic attempt.

That hope expressed itself in a prayer. Not a prayer in Greek, the formal language of the period, but a prayer in Aramaic, the language of Jesus himself.

14. Maranatha
Didache 10:5-6

The rest of the Jesus party got away, and made it safely back to Galilee. Was the whole thing over with? The Davidic attempt had not come off; the leader was dead. It was at this point that Peter had some sort of vision of Jesus in Heaven, from which he would later return, not as King of Israel, but as Lord of the Last Days, judging the world. In that new hope, the movement continued. It continued to spread and to attract new believers. And a simple one-word Aramaic prayer, that the Last Days would come soon, was added to every Christian observance, every occasion when believers met together.

Maranatha: "Come, Lord."

In the Prayer over the Broken Bread, said during the Thanksgiving Meal, Maranatha recurs as the final line. Here is the Thanksgiving prayer as it is given in the Didache, a manual of advice for the elders of the local churches.[1]

" Remember, Lord, your church, to save her from every evil, and to perfect her in your love, and to gather her together from the four winds, the sanctified into your Kingdom which you prepared for her; because yours is the power and the glory forever."

"May grace come, and may this world pass away! Hosanna to the God of David![2] If anyone is holy, let him come! If anyone is not, let him repent!"

"Maranatha! Amen!"

———————•••••———————

[1]For more on the Didache, and this particular prayer, see Chapter 16, page 46.

[2]"God of David" is an idea common to the Didache and the early layers of Mark. Mark 11:9 thus describes Jesus' entry into Jerusalem, "And they that went before, and they that followed, cried, Hosanna, Blessed is he that cometh in the name of the Lord; Blessed is the kingdom that cometh, of our father David; Hosanna in the highest."

Reflections

The death of Jesus was the end of the Jesus movement in its original sense. The vision of Peter was the moment at which Christianity, the thing which was born out of the ashes of the original Messianic hope, began to exist.[3]

The hope of a final judgement, at which the faithfulness of the believers would be rewarded by their salvation, had always been part of the program; indeed, it was its central feature. Without righteous individuals, there could have been no righteous Israel, and thus no return of God to the nation of Israel. The elimination of the national hope left the individual hope still intact. But the movement leader needed somehow to figure as part of that hope. The vision of Jesus, no longer presiding over a restored Israel, but instead presiding over the final Judgement, not only maintained Jesus in the expectation of his followers, it did so in a way that was even better, because simpler, than the old one.

What would Jesus' Return be like? There were many different conceptions. One conception, written into Mark a few years later, went like this:

> But in those days, after that tribulation, the sun shall be darkened, and the moon shall not give her light, and the stars shall be falling from Heaven, and the powers that are in the heavens shall be shaken. And then shall they see the Son of Man coming in clouds with great power and glory. And then shall he send forth the angels, and shall gather together his elect from the four winds, from the uttermost part of the earth to the uttermost part of Heaven. (Mk 13:24-27)

Thus it was envisioned, and thus it was prayed for.

Apart from that shared expectation, what else was shared by the Alpha Christians? They were a sect within Judaism, but disapproved by other Jews. They were thrown together by their belief and by the opposition to it. How should they manage? That question was answered by an early circular letter which was sent to all the churches, everywhere in the Mediterranean world.

---

[3]That vision is not recorded in any Christian text. In Mark, it is promised by Jesus, and the promise is repeated by an angel, that the disciples will see Jesus again in Galilee The text of Mark breaks off before that episode can be narrated. Matthew attempts to supply the seemingly missing ending of Mark (in Mt 28:16-20), but does not give Peter a special role; the disciples as a group are merely told to preach. Someone, perhaps with an eye on Matthew, later supplied an ending for Mark (now Mk 16:9-20), but this too falls short, and ends with the same command to preach. The Gospel of Peter puts the key disciples in a boat, about to be surprised by seeing Jesus, but the manuscript is torn off at just that point. A later addition to the Gospel of John (Jn 21) puts the key disciples (plus two who were special to that Gospel) in a boat, setting out to fish, and then meeting Jesus on the shore, but Jesus just puts Peter in charge of the Church, and predicts his death. Every text which might record Peter's vision ends before it does so. Most mysterious.

15. The Churches
The Epistle of Jacob, minus later additions

The Gospels give us stories about Jesus. But what about some advice on the problems of living together as a community? Jesus' disciple Levi of Alphaeus, a tax collector and thus experienced in administration, died early. He was replaced by his brother Jacob,[1] who from then on coordinated the Galilee part of the movement. From that base in Capernaum, he sent out a letter to the churches: the gatherings of "brethren," members of the new family of the saved, which met in somebody's home, or maybe the local synagogue. This letter Jacob updated now and then, to keep up with new isues as they arose. These included opposition from the outside as well as friction from within. Jacob's circular Epistle is the longest primary document of Alpha Christianity.

The Epistle gives a vivid sense of what it was like in those early churches. The core is here separated from the later additions, and presented entire.

[OPENING SALUTATION]
Jacob, a servant of God, to the twelve tribes of the Dispersion, greeting.

[STEADFASTNESS IN TRIALS]
Count it all joy, my brethren, when ye fall into manifold temptations; knowing that the proving of your faith worketh patience. And let patience have [its] perfect work, that ye may be perfect and entire, lacking in nothing. But if any of you lacketh wisdom, let him ask of God, who giveth to all liberally and upbraideth not; and it shall be given him. But let him ask in faith, nothing doubting: for he that doubteth is like the surge of the sea driven by the wind and tossed. For let not that man think that he shall receive anything of the Lord; a doubleminded man, unstable in all his ways.

Blessed is the man that endureth temptation; for when he hath been approved, he shall receive the crown of life, which [the Lord] promised to them that love him. Let no man say when he is tempted, I am tempted of God; for God cannot be tempted with evil, and he himself tempteth no man: but each man is tempted, when he is drawn away by his own lust, and enticed. Then the lust, when it hath conceived, beareth sin: and the sin, when it is fullgrown, bringeth forth death. Be not deceived, my beloved brethren. Every good gift and every perfect gift is from above, coming down from the Father of lights, with whom can be no variation, neither shadow that is cast by turning. Of his own will he brought us forth by the Word of truth, that we should be a kind of first fruits of his creatures.

[1] In English Bibles "James," but these people were all Jews, and their names reflect that fact. It is not our job to relocate them in another culture.

[AGAINST ANGER]

Ye know [this], my beloved brethren. But let every man be swift to hear, slow to speak, slow to wrath; for the wrath of man worketh not the righteousness of God. Wherefore putting away all filthiness and overflowing of wickedness, receive with meekness the implanted Word, which is able to save your souls.

If any man thinketh himself to be religious, while he bridleth not his tongue but deceiveth his heart, this man's religion is vain. Pure religion and undefiled before our God and Father is this, to visit the fatherless and widows in their affliction, [and] to keep oneself unspotted from the world.

[EQUALITY OF PERSONS]

My brethren, hold not the faith with respect of persons. For if there come into your synagogue a man with a gold ring, in fine clothing, and there come in also a poor man in vile clothing; and ye have regard to him that weareth the fine clothing, and say, Sit thou here in a good place; and ye say to the poor man, Stand thou there, or sit under my footstool; Do ye not make distinctions among yourselves, and become judges with evil thoughts? Hearken, my beloved brethren; did not God choose them that are poor as to the world [to be] rich in faith, and heirs of the kingdom which he promised to them that love him? But ye have dishonored the poor man.

Howbeit if ye fulfil the royal law, according to the scripture, Thou shalt love thy neighbor as thyself, ye do well: but if ye have respect of persons, ye commit sin, being convicted by the law as transgressors. For whosoever shall keep the whole law, and yet stumble in one [point], he is become guilty of all. For he that said, Do not commit adultery, said also, Do not kill. Now if thou dost not commit adultery, but killest, thou art become a transgressor of the law. So speak ye, and so do, as men that are to be judged by a law of liberty. For judgment [is] without mercy to him that hath showed no mercy: mercy glorieth against judgment.

[AGAINST JUDGING OTHERS]

Be not many teachers, my brethren, knowing that we shall receive heavier judgment. For in many things we all stumble. If any stumbleth not in word, the same is a perfect man, able to bridle the whole body also. Now if we put the horses' bridles into their mouths that they may obey us, we turn about their whole body also. Behold, the ships also, though they are so great and are driven by rough winds, are yet turned about by a very small rudder, whither the impulse of the steersman willeth. So the tongue also is a little member, and boasteth great things. Therewith bless we the Lord and Father; and therewith curse we men, who are made after the likeness of God: out of the same mouth cometh forth blessing and cursing. My brethren, these things ought not so to be. Doth the fountain send forth from the same opening sweet and bitter? Can a fig tree, my brethren, yield olives, or a vine figs? Neither [can] salt water yield sweet.

Who is wise and understanding among you? Let him show by his good life his works in meekness of wisdom. But if ye have bitter jealousy and faction in your heart, glory not and lie not against the truth. This wisdom is not [a wisdom] that cometh down from above, but is earthly, sensual, devilish. For where jealousy and faction are, there is confusion and every vile deed. But the wisdom that is from above is first pure, then peaceable, gentle, easy to be entreated, full of mercy and good fruits, without variance, without hypocrisy. And the fruit of righteousness is sown in peace for them that make peace.

Speak not one against another, brethren. He that speaketh against a brother, or judgeth his brother, speaketh against the law, and judgeth the law; but if thou judgest the law, thou art not a doer of the law, but a judge. One [only] is the lawgiver and judge, [even] he who is able to save and to destroy: but who art thou that judgest thy neighbor?

[PATIENCE IN AWAITING THE END]

Be patient therefore, brethren, until the coming of the Lord. Behold, the husbandman waiteth for the precious fruit of the earth, being patient over it, until it receive the early and latter rain. Be ye also patient; establish your hearts: for the coming of the Lord is at hand. Murmur not, brethren, one against another, that ye be not judged: behold, the judge standeth before the doors. Take, brethren, for an example of suffering and of patience, the prophets who spake in the name of the Lord. Behold, we call them blessed that endured; ye have heard of the patience of Job, and have seen the end of the Lord, how that the Lord is full of pity, and merciful.

But above all things, my brethren, swear not, neither by the heaven, nor by the earth, nor by any other oath: but let your yea be yea, and your nay, nay; that ye fall not under judgment.

[MUTUAL SUPPORT IN THE COMMUNITY]

Is any among you suffering? Let him pray. Is any cheerful? Let him sing praise. Is any among you sick? Let him call for the elders of the church; and let them pray over him, anointing him with oil in the name of the Lord: and the prayer of faith shall save him that is sick, and the Lord shall raise him up; and if he have committed sins, it shall be forgiven him. Confess therefore your sins one to another, and pray one for another, that ye may be healed. The supplication of a righteous man availeth much in its working. Elijah was a man of like passions with us, and he prayed fervently that it might not rain; and it rained not on the earth for three years and six months. And he prayed again; and the heaven gave rain, and the earth brought forth her fruit.

[THE ERRING BROTHER]

My brethren, if any among you err from the truth, and one convert him, let him know, that he who converteth a sinner from the error of his way shall save a soul from death, and shall cover a multitude of sins.

Reflections

Luther hated this Epistle; many have called it "merely Jewish." And with good reason: it does not preach the Atonement Christianity of Luther, an idea which came later. We here see the earliest churches, being strengthened in their hope of salvation, and taught how to live forgivingly with each other

Luther has brought up the question of theology, and there are several things to be noticed in that category. Here are a few of them.

• **Temptations**. God does not tempt, and neither does Satan. There is no Satan, no cosmic dualistic drama. Our own fleshly desires lead us astray.

• **Anger**. This is the great enemy of communal identity. The most general cure is humility, and the basic form of humility is humility before God, just as Micah had long ago said.

• **Social Differences**. Mixing social and income levels is a severe test of communal spirit. Love your neighbor as yourself; look not inward at your importance, but outward, at the other's need. This "royal law" can be traced to Leviticus 19:18 (and much in Jacob comes from Leviticus). Jesus states it again at Mark 12:31.

• **One Law**. The law (even in the reduced form taught by Jesus) is one; if you violate any part of it, you are a lawbreaker and sinner. For example, however chaste you may be, if you kill someone, you are a lawbreaker. And so on, through the rest of the six commandments.

• **Judging**. It is forbidden, not only as the source of harmful distinctions among the brethren, but more basically because it is God who will judge. We are not to take over the function of God. We are to walk humbly.

• **Steadfastness**. No matter how early we think this letter was, there will always be impatience at the delayed coming of the End Day, and if that promise seems not to be kept, doubt will arise about the whole system.

• **Elijah**. All that these earliest Christians had, besides the words and example of Jesus, was their common Jewish heritage, and when they are in need of an example, they turn to the Hebrew Scriptures.

• **The Erring Brother**. Opinions will change in later years, and it will be doubted that a believer, once he has fallen away, can ever be redeemed. This is a part of the general hardening of doctrine which took place as the century wore on. Here a more positive line is taken. Not only so, but good deeds such as reclaiming an erring brother can compensate for bad deeds. Here is a better way of dealing with sin; one that gives virtue, not just sin, a place in the scheme of salvation.

And much more. Jacob's advice shows understanding of the ways of God, and no less of the ways of men who are trying to live at peace with each other, in a novel, and also a threatened, situation.

So much for the community as such. But what about those *in charge* of it? Was there something that addressed their special concerns?

16. The Elders
Didache 6-12

The Epistle of Jacob provided guidance for the community. But who speaks to the elders, those who are in charge of the community? Answer: the Didache, an early text long lost and only recently rediscovered..

The Didache began as a guide for the conduct of ceremonials and other church business. It prescribes for food, baptism, and the Eucharist, and takes up some problems with visiting Apostles. Apostles were welcome, but it was easy to visit some church, pose as an apostle, and get free food and lodging. Rules are given for detecting these phonies. Later on, to adapt to changing times, the Didache added a Two Ways treatise[1] at its head, and attached an Apocalypse prediction, modeled on that of Matthew, at its tail.[2] Snippets of Matthew (and a few from Luke) were also added to the body of the text. All this has to be ignored if we are to see what the first guidebook looked like. Subheads [in brackets] have been added, and points in common with the Gospel of Mark will be noticed as we proceed.

[INTRODUCTORY WARNING][3]

See to it that no one leads you astray from this way of teaching, since he is teaching you apart from God. For, on the one hand, if you are able to bear the whole yoke of the Lord, you will be perfect, But if, on the other hand, you are not able, that which you are able, do this.[4]

[FOOD]

Concerning Food, bear that which you are able, but from the food sacrificed to idols, especially keep away, for it is the worship of dead gods.

[BAPTISM]

Concerning Baptism, baptize this way. After you have said all these things beforehand, immerse in the name of the Father, and of the Son, and of the Holy Spirit in flowing water. But if you do not have flowing water, immerse in another water, and if you are not able to so in cold, in warm; and if you should have neither, pour water on the head three times in the name of the Father, and of the Son, and of the Holy Spirit.[5]

---

[1] The Two Ways (Didache 1-5) is based on a Jewish prayer of atonement, a list of 22 sins for which God's forgiveness is asked. For details, see Brooks **Two Ways**.

[2] Didache 16. For details, see Brooks **Didache**.

[3] The translation is adapted from William Varner, with the author's permission.

[4] The sense of making do under inadequate conditions occurs throughout the text.

[5] This is the first appearance in Christian writings of the "Father, Son, Holy Spirit" formula. It is not yet the later Trinity doctrine, for which see Chapter 66.

[THE THANKSGIVING MEAL]

Concerning the Thanksgiving Meal, give thanks this way. First, concerning the cup: "We give you thanks, our Father, for the holy vine of your servant David, which you revealed to us through your servant Jesus. To you is the glory forever."

And Concerning the Broken Bread: "We give you thanks, our Father, for the life and knowledge which you revealed to us through your servant Jesus.[6] To you is the glory forever. Just as this bread was scattered over the mountains, and was gathered together and became one, in this way may your church be gathered together from the ends of the earth into your Kingdom.[7] Because yours is the glory and the power, through Jesus Christ forever."

And let no one eat or drink from your thanksgiving meal except those baptized in the name of the Lord.[8]

And after being filled, give thanks in this way:

"We give you thanks, holy Father, for your holy name, which you have caused to dwell in our hearts, and for the knowledge and faith and immortality which you revealed to us through your servant Jesus. To you is the glory forever."

"You, almighty Master, created all things for the sake of your name. Both food and drink you have given to people for enjoyment, in order that they might give thanks. But to us you have graciously bestowed spiritual food and drink and eternal life through your servant. Before all things, we give you thanks because you are powerful; to you is the glory forever."

"Remember, Lord, your church, to save her from every evil, and to perfect her in your love, and to gather her together from the four winds, the sanctified into your Kingdom which you prepared for her; because yours is the power and the glory forever."

"May grace come, and may this world pass away! Hosanna to the God of David![9] If anyone is holy, let him come! If anyone is not, let him repent!"

"Maranatha![10] Amen!"

But allow the prophets to give thanks as much as they wish.

---

[6] Jesus is thanked not for his death, but for his teaching about the Way to life.

[7] A similar ingathering of the saved "from the four winds" is at Mark 13:27.

[8] There is no suggestion that the uncircumcised are to be excluded. An affirmation of repentance and faith, which is made at baptism, is the only criterion of holiness.

[9] For "God of David" see again the note to Chapter 14.

[10] For this Aramaic prayer, see Chapter 14.

Therefore, whoever teaches you all these things said previously, receive him. If, on the other hand, the one teaching, if he has been turned, and should teach another doctrine, for the destroying of those things, do not listen to him. But if it is for the bringing of righteousness and knowledge of the Lord, receive him as the Lord!

[THE VISITING APOSTLES]

And Concerning the Apostles and Prophets in accord with the decree of the gospel,[11] act thus:

Every apostle coming to you, let him be received as the Lord, but he will not remain except for one day, and if there is need, also another, but if ever he should remain three, he is a false prophet. And when he departs, let the apostle take nothing except bread [that he needs] until he is [next] lodged. If, however, he asks for money, he is a false prophet.

And every prophet speaking in the Spirit you should not test or judge, for every sin will be forgiven, but this sin will not be forgiven. But not everyone speaking in the Spirit is a prophet, but only if he has the behavior of the Lord.[12] Therefore, from their behavior will be known the false prophet and the prophet.

And every prophet ordering a table in the Spirit, will not eat from it, but if he does, he is a false prophet. And every prophet teaching the truth, if he does not do what he preaches, he is a false prophet.

And every prophet who has been put to the test and is genuine, and who acts for the earthly mystery of the church, but not teaching to do what he himself does, he shall not be judged by you, for he has his judgement from God, for so the ancient prophets also acted. But whosoever should say in the Spirit, "Give me silver," or any other thing, you will not listen to him. But if he should say to give to others in need, let no one judge him.[13]

And everyone coming in the name of the Lord, let him be received, and then, having put him to the test, you will know, for you will have understanding of right and left.

———————··•··———————

[11]Not here a written text, but the teaching as apostolically preached. For this general use of the word "gospel," see Mark 1:14f, 10:29, 13:10, and 14:9. A similar warning about false apostles is given in Mark 13:5-6.

[12]Speaking in tongues, or "in the spirit," was characteristic of some early churches. Its abuse was always possible, and here is a warning to that effect.

[13]Doctrinal reliability is the final test of the genuine Apostle. Notice that the line between true and false is also that between concern for others and concern for oneself.

Reflections

Over time, this text not only extended itself to provide for apostles staying longer than three days (as Paul regularly did), and even taking up residence, but for the creation of permanent bishops and deacons. This takes us past the end of the Apostolic period, and into the late 60's and 70's. By the end, the Didache thus acquired for itself a second function, as something like a Gospel, with Matthew as its chief model. Like so many authority texts, the Didache evolved.

It covers not a *point* in history, but a *span* of history.

The church order texts, of which this is the earliest known specimen, are of great importance, but in very technical ways, for which we cannot here pause. Here, mostly repeated from the notes, are a few points of interest:

- **In the Spirit**. Speaking in tongues, or in a mode of prophecy, was common in the churches of Paul, and it is recognized here. Speaking in tongues is not however accepted as an absolute sign of genuineness.

- **David**. The respect for Davidic tradition is very prominent. Jesus had aligned himself with that tradition, with a seemingly unfortunate outcome, but fortunate or not, that close connection continues here.

- **Jesus**. The absence of any value placed on Jesus' death is what makes this clearly an Alpha text. Jesus here is a teacher, not an intercessor, or someone whose return from death prefigures our own salvation. The good apostle teaches "righteousness," that is, obedience to the law of God (as much clarified by Jesus). This Christianity is still close to Judaism.

- **Fixed Prayers**, like those specified for the Eucharist, were not a feature of the earliest Jesus movement, but were probably copied, like baptism itself, from those of the Baptist movement. Their elaboration here shows a considerable sacramental development: the ritual itself acquires power. But still more powerful are the Spirit-inspired prayers of the Prophets, who may "give thanks as much as they wish."

- **The Church**. Spoken of as singular, even though these are separate little meetings connected only by rare apostolic visits. The *administrative* unity of the Jesus movement's separate churches would come much later.[14]

Jesus is here seen as one gratefully remembered, as the Teacher who has put his followers on the right path to salvation; a salvation which they eagerly awaited. For that judgement, as we have seen, the members prayed with a single word: Maranatha, "Come, Lord."

Besides the delayed Coming of the Lord, there were increasing difficulties for the believers, in simply maintaining themselves in the present world.

[14]For the beginning of that development, see Chapter 61.

17. The Patrons
Mark 15:40-41

During his lifetime, Jesus went about Galilee preaching and healing, nearly always accompanied by three disciples (Peter and the two sons of Zebedee, Jacob and John) out of the five he called individually.[1] We see them in a series of vignettes in Mark, with no hint how they got from one healing or preaching to the next. A worldly-wise person might think of asking, Who paid the bills? That can be answered by following up a hint in a passage in Mark, the one which introduces the later Empty Tomb scene:

And there were also women beholding from afar, among whom were Mary Magdalene, and Mary the mother of Jacob the less and of Joses, and Salome, who, when he was in Galilee, followed him and ministered unto him, and many other women that came up with him unto Jerusalem.

———•••••———

---

[1]Mk 1:16-20 (Peter and Andrew and the Zebedees) and 2:14 (Levi of Alphaeus). The Twelve are a later development (passages mentioning them are interpolated in Mark), and reflect a later time, a few years after Jesus' death, when the administrative needs of the movement required larger forces. Even after that expansion, there remained an inner administrative core of five at Jerusalem (see Chapter 26).

Reflections

The key here is the word "ministered." They not only accompanied Jesus, they took care of things, including the overnight expenses. That they were able to do so comes out if we consider what else we know about the three.

Of Mary Magdalene, Mark gives us no details.[2] Jacob the Less would be someone other than Jacob of Zebedee; most likely Jacob of Alphaeus, the younger brother of Levi of Alphaeus. Levi died not too long after Jesus' death,[3] and was succeeded by Jacob.[4] For "Salome," Matthew in Mt 27:56 substitutes "the mother of the sons of Zebedee." Zebedee and his sons had a prosperous fishing business, not only with a boat, but even with hired hands (Mk 1:19-20). The latter women may thus be confirmed as women of means, with the capacity to "minister" in practical ways to Jesus' Galilee preaching and healing.

Peter and Andrew had no boat; they cast their nets from shore (Mk 1:16). But Peter's wife's mother (the first person Jesus heals in Mark) had a house, in which he (and his brother) seem to have lived; if we are to trust Paul, Peter's wife could afford to go on mission with him (1 Cor 9:5). She was a woman of means, and so must her mother have been: it was the mother's house that was Jesus' headquarters in Capernaum, even as Mark's mother Mary's house was the meeting place for Jesus followers in Jerusalem (Acts 12:12-17).[5]

It thus develops that not only were the original five disciples connected with people of means, they were probably known to each other: four were in the fishing trade, which provided the chief export from Galilee; Levi was engaged in assessing tolls on dried fish and other products passing through Capernaum.

The presence of the well-provided among the first Jesus circle suggests a higher economic level than is customarily attributed to the Jesus movement. The mixture of these with the less affluent was to cause tension, even division, in some of the early Christian communities.

It was perhaps not so much the poor who were natural followers of Jesus; as those who resented the economic burden of the Roman occupation.

---

[2] I exclude Mk 16:9, part of a passage (Mk 16:9-20) which was added later to replace the lost ending of Mark.

[3] Levi figures in the apocryphal literature, but only in stories which take place shortly after Jesus' death. In the Gospel of Mary, he defends Mary Magdalene against Peter, who is reluctant to believe that Mary knows more of Jesus' thought than he and the rest, that she was, in effect, Jesus' favorite disciple.

[4] The good Greek of the Epistle of Jacob makes Jacob the Lord's Brother (though he is most often favored by the commentators) impossible as its author. Far more likely, and assumed in this book, is Jacob of Alphaeus. Like his older brother, who held a post of importance (toll collector) under the Romans, Jacob probably had a Greek education.

[5] See again Chapter 26.

18. The Departure of the Rich
Jacob 1:9-11, 4:13-16, 5:1-6, 2:6b-7

Jesus followers, being often estranged from their families, tended to form mutually-supporting communities. But the richer members might grow tired of carrying the rest, and simply leave. This happened often enough that it had to be addressed. Jacob of Alphaeus did so, in material added to his circular letter. There were several additions: a gentle reminder, then a rebuke of confidence in worldly things, later a warning, and last of all a denunciation, when the rich had left the community and rejoined the world. Here they are:

But let the brother of low degree glory in his high estate, and the rich, in that he is made low, because as the flower of the grass he shall pass away. For the sun ariseth with the scorching wind and withereth the grass and the flower thereof falleth, and the grace of the fashion of it perisheth; so also shall the rich man fade away in his goings. (Jacob 1:9-11)

Come now, ye that say, Today or tomorrow we will go into this city, and spend a year there, and trade, and get gain, whereas ye know not what shall be on the morrow. What is your life? For ye are a vapor that appeareth for a little time, and then vanisheth away. For that ye ought to say, If the Lord will, we shall both live, and do this or that. But now ye glory in your vauntings. All such glorying is evil. (Jacob 4:13-16)

Come now, ye rich, weep and howl for your miseries that are coming upon you. Your riches are corrupted, and your garments are moth-eaten. Your gold and your silver are rusted, and their rust shall be for a testimony against you, and shall eat your flesh as fire. Ye have laid up your treasure in the last days. Behold, the hire of the laborers who mowed your fields, which is of you kept back by fraud, crieth out, and the cries of them that reaped have entered into the ears of the Lord of Sabaoth.[1] Ye have lived delicately on the earth, and taken your pleasure; ye have nourished your hearts in a day of slaughter. Ye have condemned, ye have killed, the righteous one; he doth not resist you. (Jacob 5:1-6)

Do not the rich oppress you, and themselves drag you before the judgement seats? Do they not blaspheme the honorable Name by which ye are called? (Jacob 2:6b-7)

---

[1]Here is the signature Commandment Against Fraud. It is basically a commandment for the rich (who else might withhold wages?), and its existence gives us a hint about the economic background of the Jesus movement: some at least were people of means. The defection of the rich, from a mutual-support group, was thus serious.

Reflections

In Chapter 9 we had a glimpse of Mark's idea of the community of the saved. It shows the separation of Jesus believers, even from their own families. That separation is where many of the problems arose. As Jesus there says, it is the believers, not one's family, who are one's real brothers and sisters. They look to God as their higher authority; they pray to him as Abba ("Father"); they are all siblings in the eyes of God. That is why Jacob and other advisors to the movement speak of "brethren." Jacob too is a brother; they are in it together. Although, as a sort of elder brother, he has advice for them.

What the "brethren" share is a devotion to the will of God, as they have come to understand it. Nothing else really exists. Jacob tries to bring them back to the idea that nothing else really exists. Especially worldly wealth.

This was a shift in the original situation of the Jesus converts. It made itself felt in these additions to Jacob's circular letter. And it equally made itself felt in a series of later additions to Mark's continually updated Gospel: the primary authority text of the early Jesus movement. They are a change in the economic as well as the theological expectation of movement members.

19. The Virtue of Poverty
Mark 10:17-31

We looked at the beginning of this late story in Chapter 4, for its statement of the Law as Jesus saw it. But the story itself goes on to add an additional requirement: believers must divest themselves of all possessions, in order to enter the Kingdom. This is Mark's parallel to the development we just saw in Jacob: the separation of the rich from many communities, leaving the poor to get by as best they could. What the movement theoreticians did was to make wealth itself sinful. The story was elaborated in two further additions, in which Mark works out these implications in more detail. Here is the original story, plus both of the later elaborations.

And as he was going forth into the way, there ran one to him, and kneeled to him, and asked him, Good Teacher, what shall I do that I may inherit eternal life? And Jesus saith unto him, Why callest thou me good? None is good save one, even God. Thou knowest the commandments: Do not kill, do not commit adultery, do not steal, do not bear false witness, do not defraud, honor thy father and mother. And he said unto him, Teacher, all these things have I observed from my youth. And Jesus, looking upon him, loved him, and said unto him, One thing thou lackest: Go, sell whatsoever thou hast, and give to the poor, and come, follow me. But his countenance fell at the saying, and he went away sorrowful, for he was one that had great possessions.

And Jesus looked round about, and saith unto his disciples, How hardly shall they that have riches enter into the Kingdom of God! And the disciples were amazed at his words. But Jesus answereth again, and saith unto them, Children, how hard is it for them that trust in riches to enter into the Kingdom of God. And they were astonished exceedingly, saying unto him, Then who can be saved? Jesus, looking upon them, saith, With men it is impossible, but not with God, for all things are possible with God.

Peter began to say unto him, Lo, we have left all, and have followed thee. Jesus said, Verily I say unto you, There is no man that hath left house, or brethren, or sisters, or mother, or father, of children, or lands, for my sake and for the Gospel's sake, but he shall receive a hundredfold now in this time: houses, and brethren, and sisters, and mothers, and children, and lands, with persecutions; and in the world to come, eternal life. But many that are first shall be last, and the last first.

———————•••••———————

Reflections

The "Verily" (in the original, "Amen") in the second addition is a giveaway. That formula is used only in the later layers of Mark, when something in the earlier teaching has come to be doubted, and the hearer is being reassured about its validity. "Verily" is thus a signature for parts of earlier belief that were later doubted. What is here in doubt is not the return of Jesus (though that too was questioned, and Jesus' Return gets the Verily treatment elsewhere in Mark), but the principle of compensation: that those who accept the community of the faithful as their real family – as Jesus was doing in Mark 6:34-35[1] – will really survive on that new basis. The departure of the rich from these communities was what challenged the community idea as it was first envisioned.

In that idea as first envisioned, one's old position in a family is replaced by a new family: the community of the like-minded. We have new "brethren," brothers in the faith (this became the standard reference within the churches). Those who follow Jesus will not lose out, except that they will have to endure persecutions during their lifetime. But in the life to come, all will be well.

This idea was later worked into a whole theology of poverty by Luke: what might be called a transactional view of life, where worldly goods are sacrificed not to be replaced on earth, but to be repaid in heaven. We will encounter his version of Christian doctrine presently.

————————•••••————————

We have been following the life of Jesus in Mark's Gospel as it was first written. He later added passages to keep his interpretation of Jesus current with recent thinking, including the divinization of Jesus. In the Beta section, we will sample those later passages, which were contemporary with the early career of Paul down to the year 45 (from which period, no letters of Paul are preserved); then Paul's own letters, which are from the Fifties; and finally the Gospels of Luke and Matthew, which, in their first form, date from the Sixties.

[1] See Chapter 9.

Beta

20. Enter Paul
Galatians 1:13-24

We now take up the best-known of those who opposed the new Jesus sect, Saul of Tarsus, who had the public (Latinate) name Paul.

What makes Paul so important? Why has he been called the second founder of Christianity? Why do his letters make up so large a portion of the New Testament? He says of himself in 1 Corinthians 9:22, "I am become all things to all men, that I may by all means save some." By his own testimony, then, everything Paul says is said for purposes of convincement; none of it is merely documentary. So his own evidence needs scrutiny. But his account of his own beginnings may be pretty accurate, and we may start there. That account was given in a letter reproaching his Galatian converts for so soon abandoning the Gospel he had earlier taught them. He passes over his conversion as simply a revelation from God (his own description of it, in another letter, differs greatly from the Road to Damascus story in Acts). But of his early opposition to the Alpha Christians, there can be no doubt. Here is what he says:

For ye have heard of my manner of life in the Jews' religion, how that beyond measure I persecuted the church of God, and made havoc of it, and I advanced in the Jews' religion beyond many of mine own age among my countrymen, being more exceedingly zealous for the traditions of my fathers.

But when it was the good pleasure of God, who separated me, even from my mother's womb, and called me through his grace, to reveal his Son in me, that I might preach him among the Gentiles; straightway I conferred not with flesh and blood, neither went I up to Jerusalem to them that were apostles before me; but I went away into Arabia, and again I returned to Damascus.

Then after three years I went up to Jerusalem to visit Cephas.[1] But other of the apostles saw I none; save Jacob the Lord's brother. Now touching the things which I write unto you, behold, before God, I lie not.

Then I came into the regions of Syria and Cilicia. And I was still unknown by face unto the churches of Judaea which were in Christ; they only heard say, He that persecuted us now preacheth the faith of which he once made havoc, and they glorified God in me.

------·••·------

[1] "Cephas" is the Aramaic form of the name Peter; both mean "rock," implying a person steadfast under pressure. Paul always refers to Peter by his Aramaic name.

Reflections

Many of the people in the New Testament are just names to us. Not so Paul. He is not only up front about himself, he is *insistently* up front about himself. His concern for his Apostolic credentials is understandable when we realize that he had never known Jesus, and was not among the Twelve who acquired administrative authority in Jerusalem, not long after Jesus' death. Paul admits that he was not among them; he insists that he never got anything from them. His commission as an Apostle came straight from God. And more than that, God had identified him as an Apostle even before he was born.

That is, he outranks them in the hierarchy of the Apostles. Or so he says.

Not the least of our problems in getting Paul straight is that Luke (in Acts) also tells us a lot about Paul, little of which matches what Paul himself says. Our problems increase: there are now two people whose word we must suspect (one of them swears, before God, that he is not lying; a most suspicious touch). Both of them seem to have some purpose of their own, in what they tell us.

Of one thing we may be sure: Paul was a Jew. Not just a Jew but a Pharisee, and thus committed to the rules of ritual which Jesus had opposed as subverting the true intent of the Law. Not only committed, but *more so than anybody else.* He stood out as zealous for those traditions. Probably this is what explains his violent opposition to the Jesus movement, when he first encountered it.

But at least one detail from Luke may be accepted: Paul was from Tarsus, the capital of Cilicia, on the southern coast of what we call Asia Minor, what the Romans called simply Asia. The Galatians to whom he was writing are the southern Galatians, near his home in Cilicia.

So Paul was a Jew of the Diaspora. He was exposed to local religions of which the Jews of Palestine knew nothing. His Judaism was zealous, but his cultural background *outside* Judaism was different. As a Christian, he has the fierce determination that is often seen among outsiders in an insider movement.

When was his conversion? The regular Apostles claimed to have seen visions of the risen Jesus soon after his death. Contentious Paul may well claim a vision in that same year, and count his years in the movement from that conversion. So when he went to Jerusalem to confer with Cephas, it will have been "three years" after Jesus' death, the year 33. His conversion may be dated to that year or shortly earlier. We will not be far wrong if we take it as 32.

So what made Paul change from zealous persecutor to zealous promoter? Paul himself suggests a possibility. But that possibility has a background, and we will first need to consider how Jesus was divinized by his later followers. How Jesus became a God.

21. The Son of God
Mark 1:21-28

Jesus attracted attention in two ways. One was his message, which (since it was anti-Roman) had to be in disguised terms; as in the Sermon by the Sea.[1] The other was his healings, of a charismatic nature, as by one who possessed, or was in contact with, higher powers. After his death, Peter and others saw Jesus as now himself in Heaven. soon to return to judge the world at the Last Days. It was natural enough for his followers to regard his earthly healings as acts of divine power, and so, alongside the stories of his healings, there were added stories of his exorcising demons: demons who recognized in him the Son of God, their cosmic enemy. This example is not an interpolation, but rather an addition: the preaching story ends, and then begins again, with new content. As is common in added material, the ending of the addition repeats a phrase, "with authority," from the original ending.

And they go into Capernaum, and straightway on the Sabbath day he entered into the synagogue and taught. And they were astonished at his teaching, for he taught them as having authority, and not as the scribes.

And straightway there was in their synagogue a man with an unclean spirit, and he cried out, saying, What have we to do with thee, Jesus thou Nazarene? Art thou come to destroy us? I know thee whom thou art, the Holy One of God. And Jesus rebuked him, saying, Hold thy peace, and come out of him. And the unclean spirit, tearing him and crying with a loud voice, came out of him. And they were all amazed, insomuch that they questioned among themselves, saying, What is this? A new teaching! With authority he commandeth even the unclean spirits, and they obey him. And the report of him went out straightway everywhere into all the region of Galilee round about.

----

[1] See Chapter 8.

Reflections

This new identity of Jesus (the Holy One of God, to hear that particular demon tell it) gave a whole different character to the evolving memory of Jesus, and required corresponding changes in Mark's official record. His original story had emphasized Jesus' long dispute with the Pharisees over small rules, and had ended with a miraculous sign from God (the Rending of the Veil, at Mk 15:38),[2] declaring Jesus the victor in that dispute. For the new idea of Jesus, something more dramatic was called for. Mark not only added exorcisms and like things, he radically overhauled the form of his story. At the beginning, the exact center, and the end, he put in voices, not demonic ones, declaring Jesus to be the Son of God. Two were voices from Heaven; the third was from a representative of Rome, the highest temporal power. Heaven and earth agreed. Here are those three moments:

• [The Baptism of Jesus]. And straightway coming up out of the water, he saw the heavens rent asunder, and the Spirit as a dove descending upon him, and a voice came out of the heavens: "Thou are my beloved Son, in thee I am well pleased." (Mk 1:10-11)

• [The Transfiguration]. And after six days, Jesus taketh with him Peter and Jacob and John, and bringeth them up into a high mountain apart by themselves, and he was transfigured before them, and his garments became glistering, exceeding white, so as no fuller on earth can whiten them. And there appeared unto them Elijah with Moses, and they were talking with Jesus. And Peter answereth and saith to Jesus, "Rabbi, it is good for us to be here; let us make three tabernacles, one for thee, and one for Moses, and one for Elijah." For he knew not what to answer, for they became sore afraid. And there came a cloud overshadowing them, and there came a voice out of the cloud, "This is my beloved Son; hear ye him." And suddenly, looking round about, they saw no one any more, save Jesus only with themselves. (Mk 9:2-8)

• [The Witness of the Centurion]. And when the Centurion who stood by over him saw that he so gave up the ghost, he said, "Truly this man was the Son of God." (Mk 15:39)

Mark's original story had been linear, and it had ended abruptly. This second version, overlaid on the first one, is symphonic. It ends with a recapitulation: a final return and the affirmation of the previously emphasized theme.

This was the first step in the divinization of Jesus. In only a few years, a second step would be taken, distancing Jesus yet further from his human past, and making him increasingly equal to God: the story of the Empty Tomb.

---

[2]Symbolically speaking, the Law and the Prophets: the authoritative tradition.

22. The Empty Tomb
Mark 15:40–16:8, omitting one still later addition

It was first thought that Jesus had ascended to Heaven at his death, like Moses and Elijah before him, and had never experienced the corruption of the grave. But shortly after the movement shifted its headquarters to Jerusalem, it began to be claimed that Jesus had been buried and had come to life again on the third day – in Jerusalem. This was discovered by women who had gone to anoint the body and found the tomb empty. In a later addition to his Gospel, Mark told the new story this way. Jesus has just died, and we are at the cross:

And there were also women beholding from afar, among whom were both Mary Magdalene, and Mary the mother of Jacob the Less and Joses, and Salome, who when he was in Galilee followed him and ministered unto him, and many other women that came up with him unto Jerusalem.

And when even was now come, because it was the Preparation, that is, the day before the Sabbath, there came Joseph of Arimathea, a councillor of honorable estate, who also himself was looking for the Kingdom of God, and he boldly went in unto Pilate, and asked for the body of Jesus. And Pilate wondered if he were already dead, and calling unto him the centurion, he asked him whether he had been any while dead. And when he learned it of the centurion, he granted the corpse to Joseph. And he brought a linen cloth, and taking him down, wound him in the linen cloth and laid him in a tomb which had been hewn out of a rock, and he rolled a stone against the door of the tomb. And Mary Magdalene and Mary the mother of Joses beheld where he was laid.

And when the Sabbath was past, Mary Magdalene, and Mary the mother of Jacob, and Salome, brought spices, that they might come and anoint him. And very early on the first day of the week, they come to the tomb when the sun was risen. And they were saying among themselves, Who shall roll away for us the stone from the door of the tomb? And looking up, they see that the stone is rolled back, for it was exceeding great. And entering into the tomb, they saw a young man sitting on the right side, arrayed in a white robe, and they were amazed. And he saith unto them, Be not amazed. Ye seek Jesus the Nazarene, who hath been crucified. He is risen, he is not here; behold the place where they laid him. And they went out, for trembling and astonishment had come upon them, and they said nothing to anyone, for they were afraid.

Reflections

Mark breaks off at this point, before completing the Empty Tomb story.

Adela Yarbro Collins has noted the likelihood that the Empty Tomb story was not present in the earliest form of Mark's Passion Narrative.[1] That may be confirmed from other evidence in the text. Four times in Mark, Jesus predicts his Resurrection after three days; the prediction which is fulfilled in the Empty Tomb story. Those predictions are closely associated with the Empty Tomb, and make no sense unless there is an Empty Tomb Story. If that story goes, so do the predictions. In addition, one of those predictions, simply by the fact that it interrupts the surrounding text, must be an interpolation. Here it is:

Mk 9:30. And they went forth from thence, and passed through Galilee, [31a] and he would not that any man should know it.

[31b] For he taught his disciples, and said unto them, The Son of Man is delivered up into the hands of men, and they shall kill him, and when he is killed, after three days he shall rise again. [32] But they understood not the saying, and were afraid to ask him.

[33] And they came to Capernaum, and when he was in the house he asked them, What were ye reasoning on the way? [34] But they held their peace, for they had disputed one with another on the way, who was the greatest. [35] And he sat down, and called the Twelve, and he saith unto them, If any man would be first, he shall be last of all, and servant of all.

So what happened? Either (1) the disciples had argued who was the greatest, a discussion unheard by Jesus, who has to ask them; or (2) Jesus taught them about his death and resurrection, in which case he knows what happened, and the 9:33 question is absurd.[2]

We can cure the absurdity by removing 9:31b-32. That is basic philology. If one of the predictions is interpolated, all four must be late. We have thus discovered that the whole concept of the Resurrection is late in Mark's text, *and thus also late in the history of Christian ideas about Jesus.*

Its reason for being is obvious. It was attractive to potential believers, as giving divine attributes to Jesus. Not only to Jews, but equally so to Gentiles, those already familiar with cults based on the idea of a dying and reviving god. It made sense to them, as arguments based on the Hebrew Scriptures did not.

Paul was a Jew of the Diaspora; he had been long exposed to such cults. The effect on him, when the Jesus sect first began to speak of itself in this way, was tremendous.

---

[1] For her reconstruction, see Yarbro Collins **Mark**, page 819.
[2] For further details, see Brooks **Resurrection**.

23. Paul's Conversion
Romans 7:7-25

The inner agony of Paul consisted of this: the Law was supreme, but the Law, expanded to hundreds of increasingly fine rules, could not be kept in full. Given the desires of the flesh, some sin was certain. All sins were offenses against God, and all brought death. This was terrifying to a devout Pharisee, since the Pharisees believed in an afterlife. For them, eternal suffering loomed.

Paul has left a picture of what this dilemma had felt like.

What shall we say then? Is the law sin? God forbid. Howbeit, I had not known sin, except through the law, for I had not known coveting except the law had said, Thou shalt not covet. But sin, finding an occasion, wrought in me through the commandment all manner of coveting, for apart from the law sin is dead. And I was alive apart from the law once, but when the commandment came, sin revived, and I died. And the commandment, which was unto life, this I found to be unto death, for sin, finding occasion, through the commandment beguiled me, and through it slew me. So that the law is holy, and the commandment holy, and righteous, and good. Did then that which is good become death unto me? God forbid. But sin, that it might be shown to be sin, by working death to me through that which is good – that through the commandment sin might become exceedingly sinful. For we know that the law is spiritual, but I am carnal, sold under sin. For that which I do I know not, for not what I would, that do I practice but what I hate, that I do. But if what I would not, that I do, I consent unto the law that it is good. So now it is no more I that do it, but sin which dwelleth in me. For I know that in me, that is, in my flesh, dwelleth no good thing, for to will is present with me, but to do that which is good is not. For the good which I would I do not, but the evil which I would not, that I practice. But if what I would not, that I do, it is no more I that do it, but sin which dwelleth in me. I find then the law, that, to me who should do good, evil is present. For I delight in the law of God after the inward man, but I see a different law in my members, warring against the law of my mind, and bringing me into captivity under the law of sin which is in my members.

Wretched man that I am! Who shall deliver me out of the body of this death? I thank God through Jesus Christ our Lord. So then I of myself with the mind, indeed serve the law of God, but with the flesh the law of sin.

Reflections

Here was the problem, for someone whose Law forbade sin, but sin which, due to the weakness of the flesh, one could not avoid. Paul could break that circle only by stepping outside it. Jesus, risen from the dead, was the answer. God had spoken, and by means of a certified miracle: a miracle with witnesses. Paul embraced it, and in so doing, he resolved his deep inner contradiction. Jesus' Resurrection, if it was ardently believed in, *would eliminate the Law*.

How did this come to him? Acts three times describes Paul's vision on the Road to Damascus. But that's Luke's picture. Paul's own account is different: he was caught up to Heaven:

> I know a man in Christ, fourteen years ago . . . caught up even to the third heaven . . . how that he was caught up to Paradise, and heard unspeakable words, which it is not lawful for a man to utter. (2 Cor 12:2-5)

and called to be an Apostle:

> But when it was the good pleasure of God, who separated me, from my mother's womb, and called me through his grace, to preach his Son in me, that I might preach him among the Gentiles . . . (Gal 1:15-16a)

So Paul's call came from a higher authority than that of the Twelve, since their call was only from Jesus, not from God Himself. And Paul's call came not during his lifetime, like theirs, but was determined at the beginning of his life.

Paul's conversion did not reconcile him to those he had earlier persecuted. Theirs was the religion of Jesus, based on the ethical part of the Law: the original Alpha faith. Paul had been converted to the Beta version, centering on the Resurrection. For Paul (if not for everyone else), that meant abandoning the Law as a means of salvation. And so Paul remained the enemy of the Alphas. In a moment of anger, he picked up their Maranatha prayer *as a curse:*

> If any man love not the Lord, let him be anathema. "Maranatha."
> (1 Cor 16:22)

Which is to say, You have prayed for the Final Judgement; see how you like it. May the Lord indeed come, and judge you, and condemn you for your errors.

What was the importance of Paul for Christianity? He abandoned the Law, and thus forsook Judaism as he knew it, fifty years before Christianity and Judaism reached a more formal separation. He championed the Gentiles, who turned out to be the future of Christianity, when Christianity still saw itself as part of Judaism. Paul's was a spirit of opposition, not one of accommodation. He was by nature an Either / Or thinker.

Quite possibly his vehemence, his possessiveness, his unforgivingness, his larger-than-self selfishness, which are off-putting to not a few modern readers, were advantages at the time. If inner convincement is the hallmark of a leader, Paul had it more than anybody else of whom we know.

24. The Syrophoenician Woman
Mark 7:24-31

Judaism had always had a certain attraction for high-minded non-Jews, who might sit in on synagogue meetings; the Jews called them "God-fearers." They grew acquainted with Scripture. Whatever they thought of "Israel," they liked the moral part. And also the monotheism part: their world was full of weird gods, some of them worshiped in indecent ways. These God-fearers sought something more philosophically satisfying.

Jesus' message of national renewal was meant for Jews alone, since only their repentance could have any effect on the righteousness of Israel and thus precipitate the return of God. But these "God-fearers" also took note of the message of Micah: that God cares only for how you treat your fellow man, and not for a lot of sacrifices or other devotions. What Jesus, following Micah, had done to Jewish doctrine was to make it less specifically Jewish. Anyone, of any tribe or nation, might obey those rules, and so hope for eternal life at the end. Thus began what amounted to a second wildfire: the adherence of the Gentiles.

It took the Jesus movement leaders by surprise. To help them adjust, it would be good if Jesus himself could be shown as having accepted Gentiles. And so this incident was composed by Mark and added to his Gospel, to bring his "Jesus" up to date with what was happening.

And from thence he arose, and went away into the borders of Tyre and Sidon. And he entered into a house, and would have no man know it; and he could not be hid. But straightway a woman, whose little daughter had an unclean spirit, having heard of him, came and fell down at his feet. Now the woman was a Greek, a Syrophoenician by race. And she besought him that he would cast forth the demon out of her daughter. And he said unto her, Let the children first be filled: for it is not meet to take the children's bread and cast it to the dogs. But she answered and saith unto him, Yea, Lord; even the dogs under the table eat of the children's crumbs. And he said unto her, For this saying go thy way; the demon is gone out of thy daughter. And she went away unto her house, and found the child laid upon the bed, and the demon gone out.

And again he went out from the borders of Tyre, and came through Sidon unto the sea of Galilee, through the midst of the borders of Decapolis.

Reflections

Of the many stories in Mark, this is the only one where Jesus admits that someone else is right. The spunk the woman shows in refusing to be refused has been much admired. What has been less noticed is that Jesus here grants that Gentiles may benefit, at least incidentally, from his message of salvation.

Don't get distracted by the "dogs" bit. Readers of the Mishnah will recall that non-Jews really *are* outside the system of that text; not subject to the Law, and not liable to the rewards that come from following it. They are nonbeings. Mark and a few others may have accepted the Gentiles without much trouble, but some others in the movement, which until now had been wholly Jewish, had to be persuaded. This is Mark's way of persuading them: to show Jesus, however grudgingly, accepting Gentile adherents, and arouse sympathy for the woman by displaying her respect, *but also her courage*. When it comes to it, who would deny a little sick child the benefit of Jesus' powers of healing?

Nobody. That insight is the basis for the way Mark put this story together. The appeal is to the spontaneous, untaught, human sympathy of the reader.[1]

The common idea that Mark cobbled his Gospel together out of stuff he got from somewhere else meets with big trouble here. Was there a free-floating story which Mark had up to now ignored, but which, once it had become relevant, he went back and included? Not likely. He wrote it himself, going for inspiration to his earlier story of Jesus raising Jairus' daughter from a coma. Mark was the Gospel tradition's first chronicler. What he wrote, the Jesus movement of that day would read. That is why it was so necessary to update it; to have it speak to the new conditions in which his readers found themselves.

And as Gentile acceptance increased, Mark made further additions to his Gospel to register, and legitimate, that process. As his last touch, he put in a line showing that the Gentiles were not only acceptable, but *necessary*, to the plan. The longed-for End Days *would not come* until the Gentiles were in:

And the Gospel must first be preached to all nations. (Mark 13:10)

Paul had come to specialize in preaching to Gentiles, but he had trouble getting his Jewish converts to share a common meal with those they regarded as unclean, namely, his Gentile converts. This produced a crisis. The problem was the food rules, which at least some Jewish converts insisted on retaining. And so Paul appealed to Jerusalem for a ruling.

---

[1]See Mencius 2A6. The system of Mencian ethics is based on the spontaneous move of a bystander to keep a small child from falling into a well – "not to curry favor with the parents, or to earn the praises of his fellow villagers and friends;" with no ulterior motive of any kind. There is something or other fundamentally benevolent at our core, a selfless concern for others, and Mencius and Mark are both reaching out to it.

25. The Jerusalem Ruling
Acts 15:13-29

Jesus regarded no food as unclean. But at Antioch, some Jewish converts, who kept the food rules, refused to eat with Gentile converts who ignored them. Paul in the year 44, early in his career and working from Antioch, asked for a ruling from the Jerusalem leaders: Peter (here, "Symeon") and the Zebedees. This is how Acts reports their decision. The leaders have been discussing it:

And after they had held their peace, Jacob answered, saying, Brethren, hearken unto me. Symeon hath told how first God visited the Gentiles, to take out of them a people for his name. And to this agree the words of the prophets:

> After these things I will return,
> and I will build again the tabernacle of David which is fallen,
> and I will build again the ruins thereof, and I will set it up,
> That the residue of men may seek after the Lord,
> and all the Gentiles, upon whom my name is called,
> saith the Lord, who maketh these things known from of old.[1]

Whereof my judgement is, that we trouble not them that from among the Gentiles turn to God, but that we write unto them, that they abstain from the pollutions of idols, and from fornication, and from what is strangled, and from blood. For Moses from generations of old hath in every city them that preach him, being read in the synagogues every Sabbath.

Then it seemed good to the apostles and the elders, with the whole church, to choose men out of their company, and send them to Antioch, with Paul and Barnabas: Judas called Barsabbas and Silas, chief men among the brethren, and they wrote thus by them: "The apostles and the elders, brethren, unto the bretheren who are of the Gentiles in Antioch and Syria and Cilicia, greeting: Forasmuch as we have heard that certain who went out from us have troubled you with words, subverting your souls, to whom we gave no commandment, it seemed good to us, having come to one accord, to choose out men and send them unto you with our beloved Barnabas and Paul, men that have hazarded their lives for the name of our Lord Jesus Christ. We have sent therefore Judas and Silas, who themselves shall tell you the same things by word of mouth. For it seemed good to the Holy Spirit and to us to lay upon you no greater burden than these necessary things: that ye abstain from things sacrificed to idols, and from blood, and from things strangled, and from fornication, from which if ye keep yourselves, it shall be well with you. Fare ye well."

---

[1] This quote is a composite of Amos 9:11-12, Jeremiah 12:15, and Isaiah 45:21.

Reflections

The solution was that the Gentiles need respect only the food rules which were theologically relevant, plus the inevitable prohibition of sexual sins.

This report differs from that given by Paul in Galatians 2:1-10. Who to credit? Paul's claim that Jerusalem recognized his exclusive mission to the Gentiles is systematically challenged by Luke in Acts; he devotes a whole chapter (Acts 10) to making Peter, not Paul, the first to convert a Gentile – after being ordered to do so by a heavenly vision, which also abrogated the rules against certain foods. That story may be dismissed as emblematic. On the other hand, Paul in his letters is continually sensitive on the subject of his Apostolic credentials, and is probably overinterpreting. And the substance of the Acts version can be verified: concern about idol food (which had been sacrificed to gods; eating it amounted to participating in the worship of those gods), and for sexual transgressions, occupies much of 1 Corinthians (some ten years later), in which Paul deals at length with the practical concerns of the faithful.

Acts I, Luke's first version of his History of Christianity, ends with the Antioch brethren rejoicing at the receipt of the letter from Jerusalem:

> So they, when they were dismissed, came down to Antioch, and having gathered the multitude together, they delivered the epistle, and when they had read it, they rejoiced for the consolation. And Judas and Silas, being themselves also prophets, exhorted the brethren with many words, and confirmed them. And after they had spent sometime there, they were dismissed in peace from the brethren unto those that had sent them forth. But Paul and Barnabas tarried in Antioch, teaching and preaching the word of the Lord, with many others also. (Ac 15:30-35)[2]

All of Acts I is meant to show how Christianity grew under God's guidance, climaxing in this note of amity between those parties *within* Christianity who disagreed about their relation to their common Jewish heritage.

The reaction of the Jewish authorities in Jerusalem was far less enthusiastic.

---

[2]When Paul later took up the thread of his story, in Acts II, he began in 15:36 with a visit to the churches by Paul and Silas (replacing ,Barnabas, with whom Paul had quarreled). The inconsistency is that Silas had been sent back to Jerusalem (15:32). So egregious was this that one scribe inserted 15:34, "But it seemed good unto Silas to abide there," contradicting the previous text but closing the Silas gap. It is at such moments that we see a problem in a text being solved by a later copyist of that text. The problem existed in the first place because some years elapsed between Acts I and Luke's resumption of his history in Acts II. The original history ended in amity between Jewish and Gentile converts. The later continuation had for its message the separation of Christians from Jews, for which see Chapter 56 and Brooks **Acts-Luke**.

26. The Jerusalem Five
Acts 12:1-17

The response of the Temple authorities (working through Herod, who alone could impose the death penalty) to the outrageously liberal Jerusalem ruling was immediate and drastic. This is how Luke tells it:

Now about that time Herod the King put forth his hands to afflict certain of the church. And he killed Jacob the brother of John with the sword. And when he saw that it pleased the Jews, he proceeded to seize Peter also. And those were the days of unleavened bread. And when he had taken him, he put him in prison, and delivered him to four quaternions of soldiers to guard him, intending after the Passover to bring him forth to the people. Peter therefore was kept in the prison, but prayer was made earnestly of the church unto God for him. And when Herod was about to bring him forth, the same night Peter was sleeping between two soldiers, bound with two chains, and guards before the door kept the prison. And behold, an angel of the Lord stood by him, and a light shined in the cell, and he smote Peter on the side, and awoke him, saying, Rise up quickly. And the chains fell off from his hands. And the angel said unto him, Gird thyself, and bind on thy sandals. And he did so. And he saith unto him, Cast thy garment about thee, and follow me. And he went out, and followed, and he knew not that it was true which was done by the angel, but thought he saw a vision. And when they were past the first and second guard, they came unto the iron gate that leadeth into the city, which opened to them of its own accord, and they went out, and passed on through one street, and straightway the angel departed from him. And when Peter was come to himself, he said, Now I know of a truth, that the Lord hath sent forth his angel and delivered me out of the hand of Herod, and from all the expectation of the people of the Jews.

And when he had considered, he came to the house of Mary the mother of John whose surname was Mark, where many were gathered together and were praying. And when he knocked at the door of the gate, a maid came to answer, named Rhoda. And when she recognized Peter's voice, she opened not the gate for joy, but ran in, and told that Peter stood before the gate. And they said unto her, Thou are mad. But she confidently affirmed that it was even so. And they said, It is his angel. But Peter continued knocking, and when they had opened, they saw him, and were amazed. But he, beckoning to them with his hand to hold their peace, declared unto them how the Lord had brought him forth out of the prison. And he said, Tell these things unto Jacob, and to the brethren. and he departed, and went to another place.

Reflections

Jesus had personally chosen five disciples (Mk 1:16-20 and 2:13-14), and the expanded Jerusalem leadership still retained an inner core of five (the Galilee Five, though with Matthew replacing the early deceased Levi). Herod's reprisal eliminated Jacob Zebedee and Peter, evidently the first and second in command. There remained Matthew, Peter's brother Andrew, and Jacob Zebedee's brother John. Curiously enough, we know how the two vacant places were filled, from a Rabbinic text,[1] something of a hit list, which gives reasons (albeit by means of atrocious puns in Hebrew) why the newly constituted Five all deserve to die:

> They brought Mattai [to the judges]. He said to them, Shall Mattai be killed? It is written, "Mattai shall come and appear before God." They said to him, Yea, Mattai shall be killed, for it is written: "Mattai shall die, and his name perish."
>
> They brought Naqai. He said to them, Shall Naqai be killed? It is written, "And Naqi [the innocent][2] and the righteous thou shalt not kill." They said to him, Yea, Naqai shall be killed, for it is written, "In the secret places he killeth Naqi."
>
> They brought Netser. He said to them, Shall Netser be killed? It is written, "And Netser [a branch] from his roots shall blossom." They said to him, Yea, Netser shall be killed, for it is written, "And thou wast cast forth from thy grave like an abhorred Netser."
>
> They brought Buni. He said, Shall Buni be killed? It is written, "B'ni [my son], my first-born, Israel." They said to him, Yea, Buni shall be killed, for it is written, "I will slay Bin'kha, thy firstborn."
>
> They brought Todah. He said, Shall Todah be killed? It is written: "A psalm for Today [thanksgiving]." They said to him, Yea, Todah shall be killed, for it is written, "Whoso sacrificeth Todah honoreth me."

These puns[3] mask the names Matthew, Simon Zelotes, Andrew, "Boanerges" (the remaining Zebedee brother, John Zebedee), and Thaddaeus.

The reconstituted Five did not hold; they shortly left Jerusalem for work in far places: Matthew in Ethiopia, Thaddaeus in Armenia. Mark, not himself a leader but a dangerously prominent figure, left shortly for Antioch, where he accompanied Paul on a mission to Cyprus and Asia Minor.[4] The leadership at Jerusalem thereafter defaulted to Jacob, the Lord's very conservative Brother, who lasted until he too was killed by the Temple authorities in 62.

---

[1]The following translation of b.Sanhedrin 43a is from Klausner **Jesus** 29.
[2]"Naqai" reaches hard for a pun (a Scripture quote) in Hebrew. So also does "Buni."
[3]Most convincingly decoded by Hirschberg **Simon** 180f.
[4]For Mark's mission and its failure, see Chapter 27.

27. Mark at Perga
Acts 12:25 - 13:14a

Luke, well placed in Antioch to know what was going on, undoubtedly knew Paul in the early days, when Paul was working under the authority of Antioch. He knew Mark, who came through town after the disaster of the year 44, when he and the rest of the liberal leadership at Jerusalem left for other places. Mark's last addition to his Gospel was about the Gentiles; of the Last Days, he has Jesus say, "The Gospel must first be preached to all nations" (Mk 13:10). True to his conviction, Mark went to Antioch, and was included on a mission journey to the Gentiles, with Paul and Barnabas. Luke tells the story this way:

And Barnabas and Saul returned from Jerusalem, when they had fulfilled their ministration, taking with them John whose surname was Mark . . .

And as they ministered to the Lord and fasted, the Holy Spirit said, Separate me Barnabas and Saul for the work whereunto I have called them. Then, when they had fasted and prayed and laid their hands on them, they sent them away. So they, being sent forth by the Holy Spirit, went down to Seleucia, and from thence they sailed to Cyprus. And when they were at Salamis, they proclaimed the word of God in the synagogues of the Jews; and they also had John as their attendant. And when they had gone through the whole island unto Paphos . .

Now Paul and his company set sail from Paphos, and came to Perga in Pamphylia, and John departed from them and returned to Jerusalem. But they, passing through from Perga, came to Antioch of Pisidia, and they went into the synagogue on the Sabbath day . . .

————————··•··————————

Reflections

What happened at Perga? Recent archaeology[1] has shown that there were no synagogues in Perga. As late as the 3rd century, we find a rich Jew, Samuel the Elder of Perga, contributing money to the construction of a synagogue building *in Aphrodisias*, more than a hundred miles from Perga. As of Mark's visit, then, there were few or no Jews in Perga. His audience there had to make the best they could of Mark's Gospel is it had been amended at the last minute, with Aramaic words translated into Greek, and specifically Jewish customs explained. So far so good, but then Mark came to the Crucifixion scene, which *does not work* unless the hearer knows Psalm 22 by heart, and is prepared to supply its last line to complete Jesus' seemingly despairing last words.[2]

That they could not do. Psalm 22? What's that?? And Mark bombed out.

Stopping only briefly at his mother's house in Jerusalem, he went to his native shore, North Africa,[3] and to the large Jewish population of Alexandria, the people for whom the Septuagint translation of the Scriptures into Greek had been made long before; the Bible which all the New Testament writers used. Mark had been named for Cleopatra's Mark Antony, still honored in the East. He was a success in Alexandria,[4] and ended up as what amounted to Bishop. It was from the scholarly and publishing center of Alexandria that his Gospel went out to the wide Roman world.

Mark's heart was in the Mission to the Gentiles, but his pen was elsewhere. It would not be until the Second Generation Gospels, written first by Luke of Antioch, and shortly afterward by Matthew, the Missionary to the Ethiopians, that the problem of a more widely intelligible account of Jesus' Crucifixion, one not demanding a virtuoso command of the Scriptures, would be solved.

So can we believe the Perga story? A lot of what Luke tells us in Acts is symbolic, and some of it is designed to put Luke himself in a good light. Mark was a competitor, and it probably amused Luke to put on record Mark's failure as a practical missionary. But this does not mean that the story was made up. On the contrary, given what we know of Perga at the time, and what we see for ourselves about the virtuosity in Scripture which Mark expects of his readers, it is not at all unlikely.

Mark *would* have bombed out at Perga.

---

[1]See Fairchild **Perga**.

[2]For what is involved in properly decoding that scene, see again Chapter 12.

[3]Mark's father was a merchant of Cyrene; Simon of Cyrene, who was present at the Crucifixion, was not only a fellow believer, but a family friend from way back.

[4]For a summary of Alexandrian tradition about Mark, see Atiya **History**.

28. Baptism and the Spirit
Acts 18:24-26 and 19:1-9

If we take Paul's letters as witnesses to all of Christianity, then everybody in the early days spoke in tongues, and everybody prophesied. But they didn't. That kind of ecstatic Christianity is characteristic only of Paul's churches. One of its features is the idea that baptism was not only a rite of entry into the sect, but also conferred the Spirit, thus making possible those ecstatic expressions. These two passages from Acts II show the distinctively Pauline spirit baptism.

Now a certain Jew named Apollos, an Alexandrian by race, an eloquent man, came to Ephesus, and he was mighty in the Scriptures. This man had been instructed in the Way of the Lord, and being fervent in spirit, he spake and taught accurately the things concerning Jesus, knowing only the baptism of John. And he began to speak boldly in the synagogue. But when Priscilla and Aquila heard him, they took him unto them, and expounded unto him the way of God more accurately . . .

And it came to pass, that, while Apollos was at Corinth, Paul, having passed through the upper country came to Ephesus, and found certain disciples, and he said unto them, Did ye receive the Holy Spirit when ye believed? And they said unto him, Nay, we did not so much as hear whether the Holy Spirit was given. And he said, Into what were ye then baptized? And they said, Into John's baptism. And Paul said, John baptized with the baptism of repentance, saying unto the people that they should believe on him that should come after him, that is, on Jesus. And when they heard this, they were baptized into the name of the Lord Jesus. And when Paul had laid his hands on them, the Holy Spirit came on them, and they spake with tongues, and prophesied. And they were in all about twelve men.

---------------··---------------

Reflections

Apollos had learned his Christianity in the first wave of Alpha contact preaching, and his form of baptism was John's water baptism. As Mark puts it,

> John came, who baptized in the wilderness and preached the baptism of repentance unto remission of sins. (Mk 1:4)

> And it came to pass in those days that Jesus came from Nazareth of Galilee, and was baptized of John in the Jordan. (Mk 1:9)

> Now after John was delivered up, Jesus came into Galilee, preaching the gospel of God, and saying, The time is fulfilled, and the Kingdom of God is at hand; repent and believe in the Gospel. (Mk 1:14)

Baptism by immersion symbolized the cleanness which came from repentance. But it was not long before baptism itself was thought to confer spiritual power. It is this sacramental baptism that we meet in Paul. Alpha documents, like the Epistle of Jacob and the Didache, though they mention prayer, say nothing about speaking in tongues. For them, the Holy Spirit was a sense of the ongoing presence of Jesus, not a power of prophecy. The concept of baptism as conferring spiritual power may have arisen from contact with mystery religions, where the devotees (perhaps further inspired by wine) would sing or prophesy. The rite conferred contact with the god, or gave godlike power.

Luke in Acts I made Peter and Paul symmetrical; it was his way of healing the rift that had developed in his time between Alpha and Beta Christianity.[1] As part of that symmetrizing, here is Peter shown as doing as Paul actually did: amending a baptism that did *not* confer the spirit:

> Now when the apostles that were at Jerusalem heard that Samaria had received the Word of God, they sent unto them Peter and John, who, when they were come down, prayed for them, that they might receive the Holy Spirit, for as yet it was fallen upon none of them; they had only been baptized into the name of the Lord Jesus. Then they laid their hands on them, and they received the Holy Spirit. (Acts 8:14-17)

Here is how the Didache describes the administering of a water baptism:

> And concerning baptism, baptize this way: After you have said all these things beforehand, immerse in the name of the Father, and of the Son, and of the Holy Spirit, in flowing water. But if you do not have flowing water, immerse in other water. And if you are not able to do so in cold, immerse in warm. And if you should not have either, pour out water onto the head three times, in the name of the Father, and the Son, and the Holy Spirit.[2]

Nothing ecstatic here. Just a sensible accommodation for those who, unlike John, did not have a flowing river available, and needed to get by with less.

---

[1] For the most public confrontation of the two, see Chapter 33.
[2] Translation from Varner.

29. The Heavenly Jesus
Philippians 2:6-11

Two things are happening to ideas of Jesus at this time. One is a tendency to ascribe saving value to Jesus' death. The Resurrection is an assurance that believers too will be brought to life in the Last Days; the Atonement asserts that Jesus' death cancels the sins of all. Paul, though not their inventor, held them. The other is the new claim that Jesus' life did not begin with his birth; that he had previously existed in Heaven. The Gospel of John will take this further, by making Jesus present from the beginning of creation. This pre-Pauline hymn not only treats Jesus as having existed with God before his descent to earth, it attaches no value to the Cross, and it is to that extent an Alpha document, but one which has outgrown the borders of the classic Alpha position.

This hymn originated in Philippi in Macedonia. Paul, in quoting it (as a model of obedience), spoils the meter by adding a half line, to bring the Cross back into the picture. Here is the original hymn:

> He, existing in the form of God,
>> counted not the being on an equality with God
>> a thing to be grasped,
> But emptied himself,
>> taking the form of a servant,
>> being made in the likeness of men;
> And being found in fashion as a man,
>> he humbled himself,
>> becoming obedient [even] unto death,
>
> Wherefore also God highly exalted him,
>> and gave unto him the name
>> which is above every name;
> That in the name of Jesus
>> every knee should bow,
>> of [things] in heaven and on earth and under the earth,
> And that every tongue should confess
>> that Jesus Christ is Lord,
>> to the glory of God the Father.

Reflections

The first group of three stanzas recounts Jesus' descent to earth, to go among men at his Father's bidding; the second tells of Jesus' return to Heaven. His crucifixion *is not mentioned*; his return is simply a form of glorification. The "name" given him is "Lord," κύριος. His obedience to God, in leaving his divine status to be born on Earth, and his further obedience in accepting death, only make him the more praiseworthy. This lesson of obedience is the one which Paul draws from the hymn, in quoting it to the Philippians.

The trouble with historical religions is that they *are* historical. They begin at a moment in time. What about *before* that time? Was there nothing at all? Did people in those times live and die uselessly? One way the Jesus movement dealt with this was to read the Scriptures as foretelling Jesus, so he was at least *predicted* from ancient times. Mark had already done this, in a few passages. This hymn takes the next step, by making Jesus himself, and not just the predictions of him, earlier than his earthly existence. In this way, the Jesus movement became less historical, less limited by time, and reached toward the universal. We are now on the brink of hearing about the divine birth of Jesus: his arrival on earth. First Matthew, and then Luke (his second version, Luke B), will fill that in with their Birth Narratives, about fifteen years from now.

And there is something else implicit here. It is this thought:

Could we be like Jesus, not just in *going* to Heaven at our death, but rather, in *returning* to Heaven? Yes, if we too had an immortal origin; if we too had in some way come down from Heaven, then Jesus' descent and ascent would prefigure ours. What we need is to understand that *this is exactly our situation*. It is the knowledge, the discovery, of our real heavenly nature, that sets us free.

Jesus, following an ethical trend in Judaism, taught salvation by *right doing*. This is the core idea of Alpha Christianity. Paul preached *correct believing*: faith in the atoning death of Jesus. This constitutes the later Beta Christianity. We now discover a third way: salvation by *true knowledge* (Greek γνῶσις). This hymn is the first hint in the record of Gnostic or Gamma Christianity.

The hymn had existed before Paul quoted it, in the early Fifties. It probably goes back to the late Forties; perhaps just after Mark had finished his Gospel. We will be hearing more of this Gamma line of thought as we go along, both from Paul and in the Gospel of John.

Returning meanwhile to a more everyday matter: *what does Paul say* in the rest of this letter to the Philippians? What sort of things passed between him and those he regarded as his charges? What was their relation to each other? What was daily life in a Pauline church like, both for Paul and for the church?

30. A Letter to Philippi

Philippians 1:1-30, 2:1–3:1, and 4:4-7, with slight omissions

Paul had been preaching at Ephesus, and as had happened at other places, his message provoked the Jews, and led to a disturbance. He was imprisoned. His flock at Philippi had sent one of their members, Epaphroditus, to see to Paul's needs in prison. Then Epaphroditus himself fell ill, and his life was despaired of. On his recovery, Paul sent him back with this message, which amounts to a sermon in letter form. This prison letter was combined with the rest of the Philippi correspondence by Paul's editors, to make a single letter. The original of this letter must be extracted from that combination. Here it is.

Paul and Timothy, servants of Christ Jesus, to all the saints in Christ Jesus that are at Philippi, Grace to you and peace from God our Father and the Lord Jesus Christ. I thank my God upon all my remembrance of you, always in every supplication of mine on behalf of you all making my supplication with joy, for your fellowship in furtherance of the gospel from the first day until now; being confident of this very thing, that he who began a good work in you will perfect it until the day of Jesus Christ: even as it is right for me to be thus minded on behalf of you all, because I have you in my heart, inasmuch as, both in my bonds and in the defense and confirmation of the gospel, ye all are partakers with me of grace. For God is my witness, how I long after you all in the tender mercies of Christ Jesus. And this I pray, that your love may abound yet more and more in knowledge and all discernment; so that ye may approve the things that are excellent; that ye may be sincere and void of offence unto the day of Christ; being filled with the fruits of righteousness, which are through Jesus Christ, unto the glory and praise of God.

Now I would have you know, brethren, that the things [which happened] unto me have fallen out rather unto the progress of the gospel; so that my bonds became manifest in Christ throughout the whole praetorian guard, and to all the rest; and that most of the brethren in the Lord, being confident through my bonds, are more abundantly bold to speak the word of God without fear. Some indeed preach Christ even of envy and strife; and some also of good will: the one [do it] of love, knowing that I am set for the defense of the gospel; but the other proclaim Christ of faction, not sincerely, thinking to raise up affliction for me in my bonds. What then? Only that in every way, whether in pretense or in truth, Christ is proclaimed; and therein I rejoice, yea, and will rejoice. For I know that this shall turn out to my salvation, through your supplication and the supply of the Spirit of Jesus Christ, according to my earnest expectation and hope, that in nothing shall I be put to shame, but [that] with all boldness, as always, [so] now also Christ shall be magnified in my body, whether by life, or by death.

For to me to live is Christ, and to die is gain. But if to live in the flesh, – [if] this shall bring fruit from my work, then what I shall choose I know not. But I am in a strait betwixt the two, having the desire to depart and be with Christ; for it is very far better: yet to abide in the flesh is more needful for your sake.

And having this confidence, I know that I shall abide, yea, and abide with you all, for your progress and joy in the faith; that your glorying may abound in Christ Jesus in me through my presence with you again. Only let your manner of life be worthy of the gospel of Christ: that, whether I come and see you or be absent, I may hear of your state, that ye stand fast in one spirit, with one soul striving for the faith of the gospel; and in nothing affrighted by the adversaries: which is for them an evident token of perdition, but of your salvation, and that from God; because to you it hath been granted in the behalf of Christ, not only to believe on him, but also to suffer in his behalf, having the same conflict which ye saw in me, and now hear to be in me.

If there is therefore any exhortation in Christ, if any consolation of love, if any fellowship of the Spirit, if any tender mercies and compassions, make full my joy, that ye be of the same mind, having the same love, being of one accord, of one mind; [doing] nothing through faction or through vainglory, but in lowliness of mind each counting other better than himself; not looking each of you to his own things, but each of you also to the things of others.

Have this mind in you, which was also in Christ Jesus:
   who, existing in the form of God,
      counted not the being on an equality with God
      a thing to be grasped,
   but emptied himself,
      taking the form of a servant,
      being made in the likeness of men;
   and being found in fashion as a man,
      he humbled himself,
      becoming obedient [even] unto death,
               [yea, the death of the cross!]
  Wherefore also God highly exalted him,
     and gave unto him the name
     which is above every name;

  that in the name of Jesus
     every knee should bow,
     of [things] in heaven and on earth and under the earth,
  and that every tongue should confess
     that Jesus Christ is Lord,
     to the glory of God the Father.

So then, my beloved, even as ye have always obeyed, not as in my presence only, but now much more in my absence, work out your own salvation with fear and trembling; for it is God who worketh in you both to will and to work, for his good pleasure.

Do all things without murmurings and questionings: that ye may become blameless and harmless, children of God without blemish in the midst of a crooked and perverse generation, among whom ye are seen as lights in the world, holding forth the word of life; that I may have whereof to glory in the day of Christ, that I did not run in vain neither labor in vain. Yea, and if I am offered upon the sacrifice and service of your faith, I joy, and rejoice with you all: and in the same manner do ye also joy, and rejoice with me. But I hope in the Lord Jesus to send Timothy shortly unto you, that I also may be of good comfort, when I know your state.

But I counted it necessary to send to you Epaphroditus, my brother and fellow-worker and fellow-soldier, and your messenger and minister to my need; since he longed after you all, and was sore troubled, because ye had heard that he was sick: for indeed he was sick nigh unto death: but God had mercy on him; and not on him only, but on me also, that I might not have sorrow upon sorrow. I have sent him therefore the more diligently, that, when ye see him again, ye may rejoice, and that I may be the less sorrowful. Receive him therefore in the Lord with all joy; because for the work of Christ he came nigh unto death, hazarding his life to supply that which was lacking in your service toward me.

Finally, my brethren, rejoice in the Lord. To write the same things to you, to me indeed is not irksome, but for you it is safe. Rejoice in the Lord always: again I will say, Rejoice. Let your forbearance be known unto all men. The Lord is at hand. In nothing be anxious; but in everything, by prayer and supplication with thanksgiving, let your requests be made known unto God. And the peace of God, which passeth all understanding, shall guard your hearts and your thoughts in Christ Jesus.

Reflections

It is interesting that the original circular letter of Jacob, which was widely known in the churches, and which Paul probably also knew, is about the same length as this letter by Paul, which Paul probably saw as a letter of instruction. It is his earliest known letter of that type. Did he learn the type from Jacob?

The hymn quoted by Paul, which brings in Christ as a model for obedience, was considered in the previous chapter. Its existence at Philippi before Paul came along means that when Paul did come, there were already Jesus followers in Philippi. And from the hymn, we can see that those Jesus followers did not have any interest in the crucifixion of Christ (Paul has to add a half line, spoiling the meter, to get that idea in). The Philippians were therefore what we call Alpha Christians. They were Alpha Christians who, by the late Forties, had arrived at a remarkably advanced concept of Jesus as not a mere man, but as a being who had existed in Heaven prior to his life on earth as a man. This represents an extension beyond the ideas of Alpha proper. It shows how ideas of Jesus were to extend themselves in various directions, in different parts of the Roman world.

Not only does Paul intrude the Cross into the Philippi Hymn, he consistently intrudes Christ into his theology. Phrases like "in Christ" which pepper this letter may often be eliminated without harm to the sense. Paul preaches Jesus, but a Jesus who increasingly takes the place of God, being himself not only the guarantee, but (in the Atonement Doctrine) the agent, of individual salvation. It is just this substitution that characterizes much of later Christianity, which ceases to be the religion *of* Jesus, and becomes instead a religion *about* Jesus.

The other person very much in the picture is Paul himself. If we go through the letter and cross out every line which is not about Paul, his feelings, his aspirations, his concerns, and his sufferings on behalf of Philippi, what is left?

This is an exercise not lightly to be undertaken.

31. Freeing Onesimus
Philemon, with one omission

We left Paul a prisoner in Ephesus. He was just about to send Epaphroditus back to Philippi. He needed help from day to day. With his string of churches, he also needed administrative help; someone to watch things at Ephesus when he was on the road. Then a fugitive slave came to him, a former estate manager in trouble with his master. Paul converts him. And seeing a chance to acquire a manager, Paul writes to the master, who was another of Paul's converts:

Paul, a prisoner of Christ Jesus, and Timothy our brother, to Philemon our beloved and fellow-worker, and to Apphia our sister, and to Archippus our fellow-soldier, and to the church in thy house: Grace to you and peace from God our Father and the Lord Jesus Christ. I thank my God always, making mention of thee in my prayers, hearing of thy love, and of the faith which thou hast toward the Lord Jesus, and toward all the saints; that the fellowship of thy faith may become effectual, in the knowledge of every good thing which is in you, unto Christ. For I had much joy and comfort in thy love, because the hearts of the saints have been refreshed through thee, brother.

Wherefore, though I have all boldness in Christ to enjoin thee that which is befitting, yet for love's sake I rather beseech, being such a one as Paul the aged, and now a prisoner also of Christ Jesus: I beseech thee for my child, whom I have begotten in my bonds, Onesimus, who once was unprofitable to thee, but now is profitable to thee and to me: whom I have sent back to thee in his own person, that is, my very heart, whom I would fain have kept with me, that in thy behalf he might minister unto me in the bonds of the gospel: but without thy mind I would do nothing; that thy goodness should not be as of necessity, but of free will. For perhaps he was therefore parted [from thee] for a season, that thou shouldest have him for ever; no longer as a servant, but more than a servant, a brother beloved, especially to me, but how much rather to thee, both in the flesh and in the Lord. If then thou countest me a partner, receive him as myself. But if he hath wronged thee at all, or oweth aught, put that to mine account; I Paul write it with mine own hand, I will repay it. I say not unto thee that thou owest to me even thine own self besides. Yea, brother, let me have joy of thee in the Lord: refresh my heart in Christ. Having confidence in thine obedience I write unto thee, knowing that thou wilt do even beyond what I say.

But prepare me also a lodging: for I hope that through your prayers I shall be granted unto you. Epaphras, my fellow-prisoner in Christ Jesus, saluteth thee. The grace of our Lord Jesus Christ be with your spirit. Amen.

Reflections

Onesimus was doubtless present when Paul converted his master Philemon. Conversions of heads of households tended to include the rest of the household, but not always slaves. Though Onesimus knew of his master's respect for Paul, he was not himself a Christian.

Somehow Onesimus came to be in trouble with his master. Since Paul offers to make it good, something about money was involved. Knowing that Paul would be an effective advocate, Onesimus fled to Ephesus (not that far away), and appealed to him. There, Onesimus was himself converted. It is on this basis – Onesimus is now a brother – that Paul appeals to Philemon.

Onesimus, which means "Useful," was a typical slave name. Paul puns on it in writing the letter, by way of defining Onesimus' higher "usefulness." The Epaphras of this letter is short for the Epaphroditus of the Philippians letter, who was still with Paul at this date, but fully recovered from a recent illness, and about to return to his home in Philippi.

The appeal was successful. Onesimus, having delivered the letter and been forgiven and indeed freed, returned to Ephesus, and became Paul's manager. He would later have a leading role in the editing of Paul's letters, and would contribute to that collection the first Deutero-Pauline letter: Colossians.

Onesimus remained in Ephesus, where he eventually became the Bishop. We will be returning to him later. Not all of Paul's cronies, as we shall see, looked with favor on this upstart intruder in their midst.

This lack of unanimity among Paul's own fellow workers had its parallel. in the lack of agreement among many who preached the Gospel in Corinth.

32. Factions at Corinth
1 Corinthians 1:10-13

We speak of "Paul's churches," but the chances are that Paul founded very few churches. Wherever he went, he will have been preceded by the earliest Alpha contact missionarizing, and followed in at least some cases by Alpha missionaries, of whom the best known is Peter. Paul wrote to the Romans in anticipation of a visit there; as it turned out, he went there only as a prisoner, to be executed, probably in 60. Peter, making a later visit, also died there, in the persecution of Nero in 64. The result of this pattern of visits by more than one Apostle was that, in Corinth and probably in many places, each Apostle had his following. Paul, who detests differences of opinion more than anyone, insists that everyone should follow only "his" Gospel, and shun all the others. That result was not easily secured.

The most famous case of factions in the churches is that of Corinth. Paul's attack on the factions at Corinth takes up the first six chapters of 1 Corinthians. Here is the passage where they are identified:

Now I beseech you, brethren, through the name of our Lord Jesus Christ, that ye all speak the same thing, and that there be no divisions among you, but that ye be perfected together in the same mind and in the same judgement. For it hath been signified unto me concerning you, my brethren, by them that are of the household of Chloe, that there are contentions among you. Now this I mean, that each one of you saith, I am of Paul, and I of Apollos, and I of Cephas, and I of Christ. Is Christ divided? Was Paul crucified for you? Or were ye baptized into the name of Paul?

Reflections

Paul we know. Apollos we have met; he was from Alexandria and thus was originally Alpha in doctrine, but had been instructed by the Paul people in Beta thinking, and was something of a Paul ally, though he took his own line. Cephas ("Rock") is Peter's Aramaic name, which Paul invariably uses. As for the faction of Christ, this is something the commentators somewhat labor over. It is at such points that the concept of Alpha Christianity is useful: Christians not distinguished by their origin (Jewish or Gentile converts), but by their doctrine: the Alpha are the primitive, pre-Resurrection followers of Jesus.[1] They follow the teachings of Jesus as he preached them during his lifetime; theirs is the original water baptism of John.

Paul's tactic in this long address is first to decry the existence of factions as such, starting with his own, and to merge all factions into a common agreement. Only later do we discover that Paul's voice will dominate that agreement:

I write not these things to shame you, but to admonish you as my beloved children. For though ye have ten thousand tutors in Christ, yet not many fathers, for in Christ Jesus I begat you through the Gospel. I beseech you therefore, be ye imitators of me. (1 Cor 4:14-16)

And be it remembered that it is at the end of this same letter that Paul curses the Alphas of Corinth, those who do not love the Lord (in Paul's specific sense):

If any man loveth not the Lord, let him be anathema. (1 Cor 16:22)

Paul's increasing insistence on his own Beta understanding reached a peak a year or so later, in his last letter, Romans. Where it provoked a public response from an Alpha spokesman.

---

[1] As far as is known, that distinction is original with the writer of this book.

33. Alpha Fights Back
Romans 3:20-24, 4:3 and Jacob 2:14-24

Before setting out to deliver to Jerusalem a donation from his churches, Paul wrote an epistle to Rome. It was not his church (he had never been there), but this was his way of summing up his theological convictions. Perhaps he had a sense (Luke in Acts says so) that he would not survive the Jerusalem visit, and that this would be his last chance to put his Gospel on record.

Paul's Gospel had come to center on the Atonement doctrine, the idea that the death of the innocent Jesus cancels out the sins of all. This idea he wrote into Romans, relying heavily on the example of Abraham's sacrifice of Isaac. In the last addition to his church newsletter, Jacob ridiculed Paul's analysis, and pointed out the centrality of good works. Jacob's response came later, but here for clarity are the two partisans, as though in dialogue:

Paul: Because by works of the Law shall no flesh be justified in his sight, for through the Law cometh the knowledge of sin. But now apart from the Law a righteousness of God hath been manifested, being witnessed by the Law and the Prophets, even the righteousness of God through faith in Jesus Christ unto all them that believe. For there is no distinction, for all have sinned and come short of the glory of God, being justified by his grace through the redemption that is in Christ Jesus.

Jacob: What does it profit, my brethren, if a man says he has faith but has not works? Can his faith save him? If a brother or sister is ill-clad and in lack of daily food, and one of you says to them, Go in peace, be warmed and filled, without giving them the things needed for the body, what doth it profit? So faith by itself, if it has no works, is dead. But someone will say, "You have faith, and I have works." Show me your faith apart from your works, and I by my works will show you my faith.

Paul: For what does the Scripture say? "Abraham believed God, and it was reckoned to him as righteousness."

Jacob: Do you want to be shown, you foolish fellow, that faith apart from works is barren? Was not Abraham our father justified by works, when he offered his son Isaac upon the altar? You see that faith was active along with his works, and the scripture was fulfilled which said, "Abraham believed God, and it was reckoned to him as righteousness," and he was called the friend of God. You see that man is justified by works, and not by faith alone.

Reflections

No one likes to think of controversy among the Christians. But there it is. It is a defining moment in the confrontation between Alpha and Beta, and the only one visible in the New Testament as we have it, without reconstructing the earlier states of some texts (Jacob *has* earlier states, but the conflict between Paul and Jacob is evident even if all of Jacob was written at one time).

Naturally, the conflict has been denied. Or it has been excused: Jacob did not understand Paul very well, or there was really no conflict between them. Thus argue the commentators. The commentators do not like discord.

On the contrary, Jacob understood Paul perfectly well. All these people lived at the same time, and they were in touch with each other, and they knew, all too clearly, what was going on.

We are not yet in the period of crisis between Judaism and nascent Christianity, which boiled up later in the century. It is only the year 57. But this confrontation within Christianity, between the older Alpha belief and the newer Beta theology, was serious. Despite well-intentioned attempts to paper it over, it eventually broke out again, at the worst possible moment.

With the writing of Romans, Paul's own letters cease. With his death, probably around the year 60, and with the death of Peter a few years later, the Apostolic Age came to an end, and the churches, and the factions within the movement, pondered what to do. One thing obviously requiring attention was to replace the Gospel of Mark, finished in 45 and now a generation out of date. The first to undertake this task was Luke, who admired Mark, but not the Atonement Doctrine which occurs in two passages in Mark. Those passages Luke eliminated. Most of the rest he kept, modifying some parts as he saw fit, and adding what he thought was most needed by the churches of the day.

This, he felt, was not more healing stories, but more Jesus teaching material.

34. The Sermon on the Plain
Luke 6:17-49

Peter had recently died, in the persecution of Nero. The Apostolic Age was over. The churches needed something better than Mark as a source of doctrine. They also needed more teaching material than Mark gave them. All this Luke provided, rewriting Mark with new additions. One enigma in Mark was the rich young man. Did Jesus really mean him to give away all his wealth? Yes, said Luke, and here is how that works. And just after the place in Mark where Jesus has chosen the Twelve, and has healed many people, Luke inserts this sermon.

And he lifted up his eyes on his disciples, and said, Blessed ye poor: for yours is the kingdom of God. Blessed ye that hunger now: for ye shall be filled. Blessed ye that weep now, for ye shall laugh. Blessed are ye, when men shall hate you, and when they shall separate you, and reproach you, and cast out your name as evil, for the Son of Man's sake. Rejoice in that day, and leap [for joy], for behold, your reward is great in heaven; for in the same manner did their fathers unto the prophets. But woe unto you that are rich, for ye have received your consolation. Woe unto you, ye that are full now, for ye shall hunger. Woe, ye that laugh now, for ye shall mourn and weep. Woe, when all men shall speak well of you, for in the same manner did their fathers to the false prophets.

But I say unto you that hear: Love your enemies, do good to them that hate you, bless them that curse you, pray for them that despitefully use you. To him that smiteth thee on the cheek, offer also the other; and from him that taketh away thy cloak, withhold not thy coat also. Give to every one that asketh thee; and of him that taketh away thy goods, ask them not again. And as ye would that men should do to you, do ye also to them likewise. And if ye love them that love you, what thank have ye? For even sinners love those that love them. And if ye do good to them that do good to you, what thank have ye? For even sinners do the same. And if ye lend to them of whom ye hope to receive, what thank have ye? Even sinners lend to sinners, to receive again as much. But love your enemies, and do [them] good, and lend, never despairing; and your reward shall be great, and ye shall be sons of the Most High, for he is kind toward the unthankful and evil. Be ye merciful, even as your Father is merciful.

And judge not, and ye shall not be judged; and condemn not, and ye shall not be condemned; release, and ye shall be released; give, and it shall be given unto you: good measure, pressed down, shaken together, running over, shall they give into your bosom. For with what measure ye mete it shall be measured to you again.

And he spake also a parable unto them, Can the blind guide the blind? Shall they not both fall into a pit? The disciple is not above his teacher, but every one when he is perfected shall be as his teacher. And why beholdest thou the mote that is in thy brother's eye, but considerest not the beam that is in thine own eye? Or how canst thou say to thy brother, Brother, let me cast out the mote that is in thine eye, when thou thyself beholdest not the beam that is in thine own eye? Thou hypocrite, cast out first the beam out of thine own eye, and then shalt thou see clearly to cast out the mote that is in thy brother's eye. For there is no good tree that bringeth forth corrupt fruit; nor again a corrupt tree that bringeth forth good fruit. For each tree is known by its own fruit. For of thorns men do not gather figs, nor of a bramble bush gather they grapes. The good man out of the good treasure of his heart bringeth forth that which is good; and the evil [man] out of the evil [treasure] bringeth forth that which is evil: for out of the abundance of the heart his mouth speaketh.

And why call ye me, Lord, Lord, and do not the things which I say? Every one that cometh unto me, and heareth my words, and doeth them, I will show you to whom he is like: he is like a man building a house, who digged and went deep, and laid a foundation upon the rock; and when a flood arose, the stream brake against that house, and could not shake it: because it had been well builded. But he that heareth, and doeth not, is like a man that built a house upon the earth without a foundation, against which the stream brake, and straightway it fell in; and the ruin of that house was great.

Reflections

This is an extraordinarily compact piece of theology. The root idea is that all ethical events are *transactional.* You are not to profit from your contacts with others (an idea already present in Rabbinic tradition, where all exchanges must be zero-sum).[1] Instead, you must seek to be always on the losing end.. *Salvation comes with worldly divestiture, not with worldly possession.*

Paradoxically, it is a lack of assurance in this world that provides the best foundation for hope in the next world. You must welcome loss, and seek to lose even more, whether it is money or personal dignity.

This is a radical departure from mainline Jewish thought, in which wealth is a sign of God's favor (it is with wealth that poor Job is rewarded at the end), and in which poverty counts as a reprimand from on high.

It is also a highly counterintuitive proposition. It could stand spelling out. In practice, does this work economically? How shall we live from day to day? If we have standards of conduct, can't we apply them to others in our group? And isn't it very dangerous to say publicly that we even *belong* to this group? Look at what happened to Peter and the other guys who preached in Rome.

Luke answers just these questions, in a long and severe second sermon, which he places later in his Gospel. The two Sermons together are most of what Luke has to offer by way of supplement to Mark, including his development of Mark's own theory of poverty.[2]

But before we take up that second sermon, we may first pause to consider one line of the Sermon on the Plain, one which it is easy to miss amid the rest. This is what has come to be known as the Golden Rule.

---

[1]For lending among neighbors, see Mishnah Baba Mesia 5:9, "And so does Hillel say, A woman should not lend a loaf of bread to her friend unless she states its value in money. For the price of wheat may go up, and the two women will turn out to be involved in a usurious transaction." For this Mishnah doctrine of *even* transactions, Luke is substituting a doctrine of *uneven* transactions: those in which the individual will be a creditor *in the next world*. Something will then be owed to him, and eternal life is the only coin in which he can be paid.

[2]See for example Mk 10:19 (Chapter 4). The implied theory of divestiture had already been somewhat developed in the later layers of Mark; see Chapter 19.

35. The Golden Rule
Luke 6:31

And here we come upon the Golden Rule, often praised as the essence of Christianity; indeed, of all religion. Whole books have been written about it. In the Gospel tradition, it first turns up as a line in Luke's Sermon on the Plain. We may now go back and take a longer look at that line.

Here is the line:

And as ye would that men should do to you, do ye also to them likewise.

Reflections

First we might ask: Is this verse at home in Luke? My answer would be No. It interrupts a series of verses on maintaining an *unequal* exchange:

6:30. Give to everyone that asketh thee, and of him that taketh away thy goods, ask them not again.

[6:31. And as ye would that men should to do you . . .]

6:32. And if ye love them that love you, what thank have ye? For even sinners love those that love them.

6:33. And if ye do good to them that do good to you, what thank have ye? For even sinners do the same.

Lk 6:31 is about reciprocity. It does not fit well where it is, or in Matthew's expanded form (Mt 7:12). It is probably a Luke B addition to the Sermon; something Luke had picked up in the meantime. Where did he get it? On its first appearance, in 05c China, it was rejected by the Confucians:

Analects 5:12 (c0470). Dž-gùng said, If I do not wish others to do something to me, I wish not do it to them. The Master said, Sž, this is not what you can come up to [it is too lofty a goal].

About a century later, it was *adopted* by the Confucians:

Analects 12:2 (c0326). Jùng-gūng asked about rv́n 仁.[1] The Master said, He leaves the gate as though he were meeting an important visitor; he employs the people as though he were assisting at a great sacrifice. What he himself does not want, let him not do it to others . . .

Analects *15:24 (c0301).[2] Dž-gùng asked, Is there one saying that one can put in practice in all circumstances? The Master said, that would be empathy (shù 恕), would it not? What he himself does not want, let him not do it to others.[3]

Analects *4:15 (c0294). The Master said, Shv̄m! My Way: by one thing I link it together. Dzv́ngdž said, Yes. The Master went out, and the disciples asked, What did he mean? Dzv́ngdž said, Our Respected Master's Way is simply loyalty (jùng 忠) and empathy (shù 恕).

Where did this interpersonal idea arise? It did not arise among the elite Confucians. It arose among the those lower down: the traders, the sub-elite Micians, whose primary philosophical tenet was undifferentiated love (兼愛). If you live by trade, you move among people of different religion and culture. The only basis for getting along is mutual trust and personal common interest. This maxim depends on no religious or cultural common ground whatever. *That is why it works.* Only the human is universal.

Nor was this Luke's only borrowing from what came over the trade routes.

---

[1]The core Confucian virtue. It is of military origin; approximately "otherness."

[2]The asterisk indicates an interpolated Analects passage. See Brooks **Analects**.

[3]Here the maxim is not only accepted, but made a central principle.

36. The Inscrutable Steward
Luke 16:1-8

In its second generation, Christian leadership expanded beyond its original Galilean home. It left the Palestinian backwater and got astride the great trade routes. This brought it into contact with new ideas, and new stories, from both East and West. Some of these stories turn up in the Gospels, where they enrich, but sometimes confuse, the rest of the story. Here is one very confusing place: the passage in Luke that has given the most trouble to commentators.

Lk 16:1. And he said also unto the disciples, There was a certain rich man who had a steward, and the same was accused unto him that he was wasting his goods. And he called him and said unto him, What is this that I hear of thee? Render the account of thy stewardship; for thou canst be no longer steward. And the steward said within himself, What shall I do, seeing that my lord taketh away the stewardship from me? I have not strength to dig; to beg I am ashamed. I am resolved what to do, that, when I am put out of the stewardship, they may receive me into their houses. And calling to him each one of his lord's debtors, he said to the first, How much owest thou unto my lord? And he said, A hundred measures of oil. And he said unto him, Take thy bond, and sit down quickly and write fifty. Then said he to another, And how much owest thou? And he said, A hundred measures of wheat. He saith unto him, Take thy bond, and write fourscore. And his lord commended the unrighteous steward because he had done wisely; for the sons of this world are for their own generation wiser than the sons of the light.

Reflections

To make a short story shorter still, here is the Chinese original (or its relevant part). This is what we find garbled in Luke:

JGT 154.[1] Later, the Lord of Mv̀ng-cháng sent out a note, asking of his followers, "Who has experience in keeping accounts, and can collect what is due me in Sywē?" Fv́ng Sywǽn wrote back, "I can." The Lord of Mv̀ng-cháng wondered at this, and said, "Who is this?" His assistants said, "It's the one who was singing, Long Sword, let's go home." The Lord of Mv̀ng-cháng laughed, and said, "So our guest has some abilities after all. But I have ignored him, and not yet given him an audience." He invited and received him, and apologized, saying, "I am wearied with affairs, and beset by worries, and have accordingly grown stupid. Being swamped by state business, I have incurred guilt with Your Honor. Does Your Honor not only not take offense, but intends to collect what is due me in Sywē?" Fv́ng Sywǽn said, "I should like to do so." He readied his carriage, put his attire in order, loaded the debt tallies, and set forth. As he left, he said, "When the debts are collected, what shall I buy with them before returning?" The Lord of Mv̀ng-cháng said, "Whatever you see that my house has little of."

He hastened to Sywē, and had the officers summon all the people who owed debts to come and match the tallies. When all the tallies had been matched, he arose and feigned an order that the debts were to be considered a gift to the people. He burned the tallies, and the people acclaimed the Lord and wished him a myriad years of life.

Driving without stop he reached Chí, and in early morning sought audience. The Lord of Mv̀ng-cháng wondered at his speed; he dressed and received him, saying, "Are the debts all collected? How have you come so quickly?" He said, "They are all collected." [He said], "What did you buy to bring back?

Fv́ng Sywǽn said, The Lord had said, Whatever you see that my house has little of. As your subject reckons it, the Lord's palace is full of rarities and valuables, dogs and horses teem in his stables, and beauties fill his apartments. The only thing the Lord's house has little of is loyalty.[2] He has ventured to buy loyalty for the Lord."

---

[1] The Jàn-gwó Tsv̀ 戰國策 is a collection of about 500 stories, put together by the Hàn bibliographer Lyóu Syàng in about the year 020 from various earlier collections. Most of them are from early Hàn (02c), but some go back earlier, to the last years of the pre-Imperial Warring States period. This is one of the early ones. It preaches giving over getting, and was thus (despite the garbling) very appealing to Luke and his church, which emphasized the value of poverty as a virtue.

[2] Yì 義, a kindness that evokes obligation ("loyalty") in return; sometimes equal to "duty" (compare δικαιοσύνη). The cornerstone of a particular kind of Chinese political philosophy, which at some points (this being one) overlaps with Christian thinking.

The Lord of Mv̀ng-cháng said, "How does one buy loyalty?" He said, "The lord possesses this insignificant little Sywē, but he does not love its people as his children, and values them only as so much profit. Your subject has ventured to feign an order from the Lord that the debts were to be considered a gift to the people, and burned the tallies. The people acclaimed the Lord, and wished him a myriad years of life. This is how your servant has bought loyalty for the Lord." The Lord of Mv̀ng-cháng was displeased, and said, "Very well. Let Your Honor now take his rest."

A year later, the [new] King of Chí said to the Lord of Mv̀ng-cháng, This Lonely One does not dare to make the former King's ministers his ministers." The Lord of Mv̀ng-cháng [being dismissed] then went to his country in Sywē. He was still a hundred leagues short of arriving, when the people, supporting their aged and carrying their young, went out to meet him on the highway.

The Lord of Mv̀ng-cháng turned and said to Fv́ng Sywæn, "That Your Honor has bought loyalty for me, today I see it."

---·····---

The manager in this story does improvident things that turn out to be, after all, advantageous. In the course of transmission it has gotten a bit banged up, and a key element has been lost. In outline, we originally had this plot:

• Magnate disprizes his seemingly useless retainer.
• Retainer gets assignment, forgives magnate's debts *in the magnate's interest*
• Magnate is at first displeased, but *later* praises retainer's foresight

In garbled form, this has become:

• Magnate distrusts his regular manager.
• Manager, still in office, forgives debts owed to magnate *in his own interest*
• Magnate *at once* praises manager's foresight.

For all the omissions and abbreviations, the basic message, the thing which recommended it to two merchants in some low Antioch tavern,[3] is still there. It appealed to them because, like the Golden Rule, *the story is transactional.*

---

[3]These things moved in both directions. We are in Bactria in the year 0326, and a Greek trader is talking: "There's this tortoise, see, and there's this fast runner, see, and the tortoise has a head start, and the fast runner sets out to catch him. Will he make it?" Chinese guy says, "Sure." Greek guy says, "No. Look here: first he has to cover half the distance, then half of that . . . and he never makes it" Chinese guy says, "Something wrong with that." But he can't figure out what. Back home, he tries it on his friends, and soon it has entered the higher Chinese culture as the paradox of secability. For the transmission of this "Achilles" paradox and other puzzles, see Brooks **Alexandrian**.

37. The Sermon on the Way
Luke 9:51–18:14

Following up his Sermon on the Plain, Luke in a second Sermon gives more detail on accepting and living the Christian life. Luke was written in two phases, A and B, and in our Bibles, the Sermon is overlaid by stuff Luke B picked up from Matthew or elsewhere. Here is what Luke A originally wrote.

Luke is the inventor of the story parable, and the Sermon has many of them. Each of its twelve thematic sections is built around a group of three sayings or stories, sometimes with a saying before or after the triplet. Subheads have been added, and the triplet members are marked, to make this structure more visible.

The counsel is austere. Discipleship is hard. It is dangerous. And it requires full commitment. But moments of encouragement are scattered here and there, to help the hearers not to lose heart on their difficult path.

[1. TOTAL COMMITMENT]

① And it came to pass, when the days were well-nigh come that he should be received up, he steadfastly set his face to go to Jerusalem.

❷ And as they went on the way, a certain man said unto him, I will follow thee whithersoever thou goest. And Jesus said unto him, The foxes have holes, and the birds of the heaven [have] nests; but the Son of man hath not where to lay his head.

❸ And he said unto another, Follow me. But he said, Lord, suffer me first to go and bury my father. But he said unto him, Leave the dead to bury their own dead; but go thou and publish abroad the kingdom of God.

❹ And another also said, I will follow thee, Lord; but first suffer me to bid farewell to them that are at my house. But Jesus said unto him, No man, having put his hand to the plow, and looking back, is fit for the kingdom of God.

⑤ Now as they went on their way, he entered into a certain village: and a certain woman named Martha received him into her house. And she had a sister called Mary, who also sat at the Lord's feet, and heard his word. But Martha was cumbered about much serving; and she came up to him, and said, Lord, dost thou not care that my sister did leave me to serve alone? Bid her therefore that she help me. But the Lord answered and said unto her, Martha, Martha, thou art anxious and troubled about many things: but one thing is needful: for Mary hath chosen the good part, which shall not be taken away from her.[1]

[1]This long piece is not part of the triplet; it is more in the nature of an addendum. When we get the end of the next section, we will see what Luke had in mind.

[2. TRUSTING IN PRAYER]

❶ And it came to pass, as he was praying in a certain place, that when he ceased, one of his disciples said unto him, Lord, teach us to pray, even as John also taught his disciples. And he said unto them, When ye pray, say, Father, Hallowed be thy name. Thy kingdom come. Give us day by day our daily bread. And forgive us our sins; for we ourselves also forgive every one that is indebted to us. And bring us not into temptation.[2]

❷ And he said unto them, Which of you shall have a friend, and shall go unto him at midnight, and say to him, Friend, lend me three loaves; for a friend of mine is come to me from a journey, and I have nothing to set before him; and he from within shall answer and say, Trouble me not: the door is now shut, and my children are with me in bed; I cannot rise and give thee? I say unto you, Though he will not rise and give him because he is his friend, yet because of his importunity he will arise and give him as many as he needeth.[3]

❸ And I say unto you, Ask, and it shall be given you; seek, and ye shall find; knock, and it shall be opened unto you. For every one that asketh receiveth; and he that seeketh findeth; and to him that knocketh it shall be opened. And of which of you that is a father shall his son ask a loaf, and he give him a stone? or a fish, and he for a fish give him a serpent? Or [if] he shall ask an egg, will he give him a scorpion? If ye then, being evil, know how to give good gifts unto your children, how much more shall [your] heavenly Father give the Holy Spirit to them that ask him? [4]

④ And it came to pass, as he said these things, a certain woman out of the multitude lifted up her voice, and said unto him, Blessed is the womb that bare thee, and the breasts which thou didst suck. But he said, Yea rather, blessed are they that hear the word of God, and keep it.[5]

[2]Here is the first appearance of the Lord's Prayer, probably as it had been prayed in Luke's Antioch church. Matthew would later pick it up, with other gems from Luke, give it a more sonorous ecclesiastical form, and pack it into his expanded version of Luke's Sermon on the Plain. The result was the Sermon on the Mount.

[3]Next, in the triplet, is an assurance that prayer works. Since it even works for your reluctant neighbor (if one persists sufficiently), how much more will it work with God? To ask God once, and then claim failure because your wish was not instantly granted, is a misunderstanding. Even the neighbor, eventually, will give you all you need.

[4]Last, in the triplet, follows a plea for trust. We do not give evil gifts to our children; still less will God give evil to us, who call him Abba, "Father."

[5]At first reading, this piece is hard to relate to what precedes. Well, it *doesn't* relate to what precedes. It relates instead to its formal parallel: the concluding piece of §1, the Mary and Martha story. That too was about enthusiasm exerted in the wrong direction. Not housework, or even motherhood, is more important than "hearing the word of God" (as Mary had done in §1) and keeping it." Another bit of parallelism is the simple fact that both pieces feature women, as Luke in general often does.

[3. THE NEED AND DANGER OF OPEN WITNESS]

❶ No man, when he hath lighted a lamp, putteth it in a cellar, neither under the bushel, but on the stand, that they which enter in may see the light.[6]

❷ But there is nothing covered up, that shall not be revealed; and hid, that shall not be known. Wherefore whatsoever ye have said in the darkness shall be heard in the light; and what ye have spoken in the ear in the inner chambers shall be proclaimed upon the housetops.[7]

❸ And I say unto you my friends, Be not afraid of them that kill the body, and after that have no more that they can do. But I will warn you whom ye shall fear: Fear him, who after he hath killed hath power to cast into hell; yea, I say unto you, Fear him.

④ Are not five sparrows sold for two pence? And not one of them is forgotten in the sight of God. But the very hairs of your head are all numbered. Fear not: ye are of more value than many sparrows.[8]

[4. AGAINST APOSTASY]

❶ And I say unto you, Every one who shall confess me before men, him shall the Son of man also confess before the angels of God; but he that denieth me in the presence of men shall be denied in the presence of the angels of God.

❷ And every one who shall speak a word against the Son of man, it shall be forgiven him: but unto him that blasphemeth against the Holy Spirit it shall not be forgiven.[9]

❸ And when they bring you before the synagogues,[10] and the rulers, and the authorities, be not anxious how or what ye shall answer, or what ye shall say: for the Holy Spirit shall teach you in that very hour what ye ought to say.[11]

---

[6]This is from Mark 4:21, part of Mark's Sermon on the Sea. Luke has already repeated this line in following Mark (at Luke 8:16-18); here, composing on his own, he uses it again. This is called a doublet. Of 15 doublets in Luke, about half represent borrowing from other places in Luke, to make up his Sermon on the Way.

[7]The rather cheerful atmosphere of the preceding passage here turns dark. This kind of witnessing to others is dangerous, and it cannot be kept wholly secret. Jesus himself, in the Sermon on the Sea, spoke in similitudes to avoid detection.

[8]This note of encouragement is appended to the triplet proper.

[9]This is from Mark 3:28-29 (Jesus' reply to those who accused him of being possessed by a demon), which was not repeated in the corresponding place in Luke; it was apparently saved out for use here. That is, Luke has planned his Gospel as a unit.

[10]The synagogues could punish with forty lashes (Mishnah Makkot 1:1-3 prescribes flogging for perjury, 3:1-3 for other crimes; see 3:11-13 for the technique of flogging). Paul recalls how "of the Jews five times I received forty less one (2 Corinthians 11:24).

[11]In Mark 13:11, this is part of the predictions for the End Days; its proper parallel is Luke 21:14-15. In this case, Luke has doubled a passage from *later* in his text, for use in the Sermon on the Way. All this shows us, in detail, Luke's way of working.

[5. AGAINST WORLDLINESS]

① And one out of the multitude said unto him, Teacher, bid my brother divide the inheritance with me. But he said unto him, Man, who made me a judge or a divider over you? And he said unto them, Take heed, and keep yourselves from all covetousness: for a man's life consisteth not in the abundance of the things which he possesseth.

❷ And he spake a parable unto them, saying, The ground of a certain rich man brought forth plentifully: and he reasoned within himself, saying, What shall I do, because I have not where to bestow my fruits? And he said, This will I do: I will pull down my barns, and build greater; and there will I bestow all my grain and my goods. And I will say to my soul, Soul, thou hast much goods laid up for many years; take thine ease, eat, drink, be merry. But God said unto him, Thou foolish one, this night is thy soul required of thee; and the things which thou hast prepared, whose shall they be?[12] So is he that layeth up treasure for himself, and is not rich toward God.

❸ And he said unto his disciples, Therefore I say unto you, Be not anxious for [your] life, what ye shall eat; nor yet for your body, what ye shall put on. For the life is more than the food, and the body than the raiment. Consider the ravens, that they sow not, neither reap; which have no store-chamber nor barn; and God feedeth them: of how much more value are ye than the birds! And which of you by being anxious can add a cubit unto the measure of his life? If then ye are not able to do even that which is least, why are ye anxious concerning the rest? Consider the lilies, how they grow: they toil not, neither do they spin; yet I say unto you, Even Solomon in all his glory was not arrayed like one of these. But if God doth so clothe the grass in the field, which to-day is, and to-morrow is cast into the oven; how much more [shall he clothe] you, O ye of little faith?

❹ And seek not ye what ye shall eat, and what ye shall drink, neither be ye of doubtful mind. For all these things do the nations of the world seek after: but your Father knoweth that ye have need of these things. Yet seek ye his kingdom, and these things shall be added unto you.

⑤ Fear not, little flock; for it is your Father's good pleasure to give you the kingdom.[13]

---

[12]Luke rarely quotes Scripture in this Sermon, which is pitched in a somewhat different voice. But here, to give the story an appropriately high tone in quoting God, he echoes Jeremiah 17:11, "As the partridge that sitteth on eggs which she hath not laid, so is he that getteth riches, and not by right; in the midst of his days they shall leave him, and at his end he shall be a fool." Jeremiah had referred only to ill-gotten gains; Luke here warns against any gains whatever.

[13]Another word of encouragement occurring as a postscript to the triplet proper. Beginning with §3, sections tend to alternate warnings with words of encouragement. This too is part of the strategy of the Sermon.

[6. WATCHFUL WAITING]

❶ Sell that which ye have, and give alms; make for yourselves purses which wax not old, a treasure in the heavens that faileth not, where no thief draweth near, neither moth destroyeth. For where your treasure is, there will your heart be also.

❷ Let your loins be girded about, and your lamps burning; and be ye yourselves like unto men looking for their lord, when he shall return from the marriage feast; that, when he cometh and knocketh, they may straightway open unto him. Blessed are those servants, whom the lord when he cometh shall find watching: verily I say unto you, that he shall gird himself, and make them sit down to meat, and shall come and serve them. And if he shall come in the second watch, and if in the third, and find [them] so blessed are those [servants]. But know this, that if the master of the house had known in what hour the thief was coming, he would have watched, and not have left his house to be broken through. Be ye also ready: for in an hour that ye think not the Son of man cometh.

❸ And Peter said, Lord, speakest thou this parable unto us, or even unto all? And the Lord said, Who then is the faithful and wise steward, whom his lord shall set over his household, to give them their portion of food in due season? Blessed is that servant, whom his lord when he cometh shall find so doing. Of a truth I say unto you, that he will set him over all that he hath. But if that servant shall say in his heart, My lord delayeth his coming; and shall begin to beat the menservants and the maidservants, and to eat and drink, and to be drunken; the lord of that servant shall come in a day when he expecteth not, and in an hour when he knoweth not, and shall cut him asunder, and appoint his portion with the unfaithful. And that servant, who knew his lord's will, and made not ready, nor did according to his will, shall be beaten with many [stripes]; but he that knew not, and did things worthy of stripes, shall be beaten with few [stripes]. And to whomsoever much is given, of him shall much be required: and to whom they commit much, of him will they ask the more.

④ I came to cast fire upon the earth; and what do I desire, if it is already kindled? But I have a baptism to be baptized with; and how am I straitened till it be accomplished! Think ye that I am come to give peace in the earth? I tell you, Nay; but rather division: for there shall be from henceforth five in one house divided, three against two, and two against three. They shall be divided, father against son, and son against father; mother against daughter, and daughter against her mother; mother in law against her daughter in law, and daughter in law against her mother in law.[14]

---

[14]In this coda to the "watchful" triplet, Jesus reminds the disciples of the dangers threatening believers, even in their own families.

[7. THE COMING END]

❶ And he said to the multitudes also, When ye see a cloud rising in the west, straightway ye say, There cometh a shower; and so it cometh to pass. And when [ye see] a south wind blowing, ye say, There will be a scorching heat; and it cometh to pass. Ye hypocrites, ye know how to interpret the face of the earth and the heaven; but how is it that ye know not how to interpret this time?[15]

❷ And why even of yourselves judge ye not what is right? For as thou art going with thine adversary before the magistrate, on the way give diligence to be quit of him; lest haply he drag thee unto the judge, and the judge shall deliver thee to the officer, and the officer shall cast thee into prison. I say unto thee, Thou shalt by no means come out thence, till thou have paid the very last mite.[16]

❸ Now there were some present at that very season who told him of the Galileans, whose blood Pilate had mingled with their sacrifices. And he answered and said unto them, Think ye that these Galileans were sinners above all the Galileans, because they have suffered these things? I tell you, Nay: but, except ye repent, ye shall all in like manner perish. Or those eighteen, upon whom the tower in Siloam fell, and killed them, think ye that they were offenders above all the men that dwell in Jerusalem? I tell you, Nay: but, except ye repent, ye shall all likewise perish.[17]

④ And he spake this parable; A certain man had a fig tree planted in his vineyard; and he came seeking fruit thereon, and found none.[18] And he said unto the vinedresser, Behold, these three years I come seeking fruit on this fig tree, and find none: cut it down; why doth it also cumber the ground? And he answering saith unto him, Lord, let it alone this year also, till I shall dig about it, and dung it: and if it bear fruit thenceforth, [well]; but if not, thou shalt cut it down.[19]

---

[15]This passage and the next are linked by the motif of judgement.

[16]The wrong of resorting to secular courts was noted in one of Jacob's hostile references to the rich (Jacob 2:6b, "Do not the rich oppress you, and themselves drag you before the judgement seats?"). The Epistle of Jacob was very widely distributed, and many later writings, whether Alpha or Beta, show signs of acquaintance with it.

[17]Is the hand of God to be seen in such random events? "Jesus" here denies it. Similar questions were asked at an earlier period in China. Mencius 7A2 distinguishes one's allotted life span from random interferences: "Mencius said, There is nothing that is not fated, but one assents only to what is right. For this reason, one who understands Fate will not stand under a tottering wall. If one die after following his Way to the end, that is a proper Fate. To die in fetters is not a proper Fate."

[18]A faint echo of Jesus's cursing of a barren fig tree in Mark 11:12-14. Luke is not above revising Mark's Jesus (who in that passage was condemnatory), and here, in the voice of a humbler figure, successfully appeals the sentence of death for the fig tree.

[19]The concluding message is a reassurance: There will be time to repent.

[8. RENOUNCING WORLDLY CONVENTIONS]

① And it came to pass, when he went into the house of one of the rulers of the Pharisees on a Sabbath to eat bread, that they were watching him.

❷ And behold, there was before him a certain man that had the dropsy. And Jesus answering spake unto the lawyers and Pharisees, saying, Is it lawful to heal on the Sabbath, or not? But they held their peace. And he took him, and healed him, and let him go. And he said unto them, Which of you shall have an ass or an ox fallen into a well, and will not straightway draw him up on a Sabbath day? And they could not answer again unto these things.

❸ And he spake a parable unto those that were bidden, when he marked how they chose out the chief seats; saying unto them, When thou art bidden of any man to a marriage feast, sit not down in the chief seat; lest haply a more honorable man than thou be bidden of him, and he that bade thee and him shall come and say to thee, Give this man place; and then thou shalt begin with shame to take the lowest place. But when thou art bidden, go and sit down in the lowest place; that when he that hath bidden thee cometh, he may say to thee, Friend, go up higher: then shalt thou have glory in the presence of all that sit at meat with thee. For everyone that exalteth himself shall be humbled; and he that humbleth himself shall be exalted.

❹ And he said to him also that had bidden him, When thou makest a dinner or a supper, call not thy friends, nor thy brethren, nor thy kinsmen, nor rich neighbors; lest haply they also bid thee again, and a recompense be made thee. But when thou makest a feast, bid the poor, the maimed, the lame, the blind: and thou shalt be blessed; because they have not [wherewith] to recompense thee: for thou shalt be recompensed in the resurrection of the just.

⑤ And when one of them that sat at meat with him heard these things, he said unto him, Blessed is he that shall eat bread in the kingdom of God. But he said unto him, A certain man made a great supper; and he bade many. And he sent forth his servant at supper time to say to them that were bidden, Come; for [all] things are now ready. And they all with one [consent] began to make excuse. The first said unto him, I have bought a field, and I must needs go out and see it; I pray thee have me excused. And another said, I have bought five yoke of oxen, and I go to prove them; I pray thee have me excused. And another said, I have married a wife, and therefore I cannot come. And the servant came, and told his lord these things. Then the master of the house being angry said to his servant, Go out quickly into the streets and lanes of the city, and bring in hither the poor and maimed and blind and lame. And the servant said, Lord, what thou didst command is done, and yet there is room. And the lord said unto the servant, Go out into the highways and hedges, and constrain [them] to come in, that my house may be filled. For I say unto you, that none of those men that were bidden shall taste of my supper.

[9. CONTINUING IN DISCIPLESHIP]

❶ Now there went with him great multitudes: and he turned, and said unto them, If any man cometh unto me, and hateth not his own father, and mother, and wife, and children, and brethren, and sisters, yea, and his own life also, he cannot be my disciple. Whosoever doth not bear his own cross, and come after me, cannot be my disciple.[20]

❷ For which of you, desiring to build a tower, doth not first sit down and count the cost, whether he have [wherewith] to complete it? Lest haply, when he hath laid a foundation, and is not able to finish, all that behold begin to mock him, saying, This man began to build, and was not able to finish.

❸ Or what king, as he goeth to encounter another king in war, will not sit down first and take counsel whether he is able with ten thousand to meet him that cometh against him with twenty thousand? Or else, while the other is yet a great way off, he sendeth an embassy, and asketh conditions of peace. So therefore whosoever he be of you that renounceth not all that he hath, he cannot be my disciple.

④ Salt therefore is good: but if even the salt have lost its savor, wherewith shall it be seasoned? It is fit neither for the land nor for the dunghill: [men] cast it out. He that hath ears to hear, let him hear.

[10. REJOICING OVER THE SAVED]

① Now all the publicans and sinners were drawing near unto him to hear him. And both the Pharisees and the scribes murmured, saying, This man receiveth sinners, and eateth with them.

❷ And he spake unto them this parable, saying, What man of you, having a hundred sheep, and having lost one of them, doth not leave the ninety and nine in the wilderness, and go after that which is lost, until he find it? And when he hath found it, he layeth it on his shoulders, rejoicing. And when he cometh home, he calleth together his friends and his neighbors, saying unto them, Rejoice with me, for I have found my sheep which was lost. I say unto you, that even so there shall be joy in heaven over one sinner that repenteth, [more] than over ninety and nine righteous persons, who need no repentance.[21]

❸ Or what woman having ten pieces of silver, if she lose one piece, doth not light a lamp, and sweep the house, and seek diligently until she find it? And when she hath found it, she calleth together her friends and neighbors, saying, Rejoice with me, for I have found the piece which I had lost. Even so, I say unto you, there is joy in the presence of the angels of God over one sinner that repenteth.

[20]Another Lukan doublet. Mark 8:34 was included in its proper place at Luke 9:23, but is repeated here as part of Luke's Sermon.

[21]Mark's Jesus (Mark 2:21) had said, "I came not to call the righteous, but sinners."

❹ And he said, A certain man had two sons. And the younger of them said to his father, Father, give me the portion of [thy] substance that falleth to me. And he divided unto them his living. And not many days after, the younger son gathered all together and took his journey into a far country; and there he wasted his substance with riotous living. And when he had spent all, there arose a mighty famine in that country; and he began to be in want. And he went and joined himself to one of the citizens of that country; and he sent him into his fields to feed swine.[22] And he would fain have filled his belly with the husks that the swine did eat: and no man gave unto him.

But when he came to himself he said, How many hired servants of my father's have bread enough and to spare, and I perish here with hunger! I will arise and go to my father, and will say unto him, Father, I have sinned against heaven, and in thy sight: I am no more worthy to be called your son: make me as one of thy hired servants. And he arose, and came to his father. But while he was yet afar off, his father saw him, and was moved with compassion, and ran, and fell on his neck, and kissed him. And the son said unto him, Father, I have sinned against heaven, and in thy sight: I am no more worthy to be called thy son.

But the father said to his servants, Bring forth quickly the best robe, and put it on him; and put a ring on his hand, and shoes on his feet: and bring the fatted calf, [and] kill it, and let us eat, and make merry: for this my son was dead, and is alive again; he was lost, and is found. And they began to be merry. Now his elder son was in the field: and as he came and drew nigh to the house, he heard music and dancing. And he called to him one of the servants, and inquired what these things might be. And he said unto him, Thy brother is come; and thy father hath killed the fatted calf, because he hath received him safe and sound. But he was angry, and would not go in: and his father came out, and entreated him. But he answered and said to his father, Lo, these many years do I serve thee, and I never transgressed a commandment of thine; and [yet] thou never gavest me a kid, that I might make merry with my friends: but when this thy son came, who hath devoured thy living with harlots, thou killedst for him the fatted calf. And he said unto him, Son, thou art ever with me, and all that is mine is thine. But it was meet to make merry and be glad: for this thy brother was dead, and is alive [again]; and [was] lost, and is found.[23]

---

[22] A country with swine is not part of Israel; the younger son has alienated himself.

[23] Early converts, especially the righteous among them, were inclined to be jealous over the fuss made when a new, and seemingly less deserving, member was added. This parable (often misinterpreted as being about repentance) is a fully worked out argument about reasons for joy. The new member does not deprive the old member (the older son) of anything; all the Father has to give is his. But the saving of a soul from what would otherwise be death should be a cause of rejoicing among the already saved.

[11. AGAINST WORLDLY WISDOM]

❶ And he said also unto the disciples, There was a certain rich man, who had a steward; and the same was accused unto him that he was wasting his goods. And he called him, and said unto him, What is this that I hear of thee? render the account of thy stewardship; for thou canst be no longer steward. And the steward said within himself, What shall I do, seeing that my lord taketh away the stewardship from me? I have not strength to dig; to beg I am ashamed. I am resolved what to do, that, when I am put out of the stewardship, they may receive me into their houses. And calling to him each one of his lord's debtors, he said to the first, How much owest thou unto my lord? And he said, A hundred measures of oil. And he said unto him, Take thy bond, and sit down quickly and write fifty. Then said he to another, And how much owest thou? And he said, A hundred measures of wheat. He saith unto him, Take thy bond, and write fourscore. And his lord commended the unrighteous steward because he had done wisely: for the sons of this world are for their own generation wiser than the sons of the light.[24] And I say unto you, Make to yourselves friends by means of the mammon of unrighteousness; that, when it shall fail, they may receive you into the eternal tabernacles.

❷ And the Pharisees, who were lovers of money, heard all these things; and they scoffed at him. And he said unto them, Ye are they that justify yourselves in the sight of men; but God knoweth your hearts: for that which is exalted among men is an abomination in the sight of God.

❸ Now there was a certain rich man, and he was clothed in purple and fine linen, faring sumptuously every day: and a certain beggar named Lazarus was laid at his gate, full of sores, and desiring to be fed with the [crumbs] that fell from the rich man's table; yea, even the dogs come and licked his sores. And it came to pass, that the beggar died, and that he was carried away by the angels into Abraham's bosom; and the rich man also died, and was buried. And in Hades he lifted up his eyes, being in torments, and seeth Abraham afar off, and Lazarus in his bosom. And he cried and said, Father Abraham, have mercy on me, and send Lazarus, that he may dip the tip of his finger in water, and cool my tongue; for I am in anguish in this flame. But Abraham said, Son, remember that thou in thy lifetime receivedst thy good things, and Lazarus in like manner evil things: but now here he is comforted and thou art in anguish. And besides all this, between us and you there is a great gulf fixed, that they that would pass from hence to you may not be able, and that none may cross over from thence to us.[25]

---

[24]This garbled story (Luke 16:1-8), which has been the despair of the commentators, was probably picked up from traders passing through the great trade center of Antioch. The Chinese original is found at Jàn-gwó Tsv̀ 154. For the connection, see Chapter 36.

[25]Luke would later return to this parable and expand it; this is the original version. For the three compositional stages of Luke, see Brooks **Acts-Luke**.

[12. SIN AND SHORTCOMING]

❶ And he said unto his disciples, It is impossible but that occasions of stumbling should come; but woe unto him, through whom they come! It were well for him if a millstone were hanged about his neck, and he were thrown into the sea, rather than that he should cause one of these little ones to stumble.

❷ Take heed to yourselves: if thy brother sin, rebuke him; and if he repent, forgive him. And if he sin against thee seven times in the day, and seven times turn again to thee, saying, I repent; thou shalt forgive him.

❸ But who is there of you, having a servant plowing or keeping sheep, that will say unto him, when he is come in from the field, Come straightway and sit down to meat; and will not rather say unto him, Make ready wherewith I may sup, and gird thyself, and serve me, till I have eaten and drunken; and afterward thou shalt eat and drink? Doth he thank the servant because he did the things that were commanded? Even so ye also, when ye shall have done all the things that are commanded you, say, We are unprofitable servants; we have done that which it was our duty to do.

④ And being asked by the Pharisees, when the Kingdom of God cometh, he answered them and said, The Kingdom of God cometh not with observation, neither shall they say, Lo, here! or, There! for lo, the Kingdom of God is within you.[26]

[26]This piece rebukes the current questioning about when the Last Days, the Final Judgement, would come. Luke puts it off. He is not a fire and brimstone preacher. He is a preacher for the Time Between: what do we do right now? The chief thing we have to do, as his Sermon on the Plain spelled out for the theologians in our midst, is to create a favorable credit balance for ourselves in the Heavenly Account Book. That is the point of the next to last piece in this section (which is also the final section, we are almost through with this Sermon on the Way of Christian Living). We must not merely do our duty, but *more* than our duty; we must be on the credit side of the ledger. What is required of us is, precisely, *more* than is required. Hard as that is, that is what it is.

But then comes a small (and perhaps borrowed) comment on that eventual Kingdom of Heaven, the thing all this is tending to. It is not solely a future one. If you are living as you ought, and treating others as you should, *you are already living the Kingdom.*

Later on, Luke B would borrow some Apocalyptic material from Matthew, for reasons that seemed good to him at the time (everybody was doing Apocalypse, and maybe Luke wanted his book to be up to the current standard). He chose to insert it after this Pharisee inquiry, which at least raises the question of the End, and anyway, the end of the Sermon is a good enough place for the End of the World. But it changes the meaning of this encouragement piece, making it difficult for readers of our present Luke to get the originally intended force of this final passage. In its original context, it may remind us of many an earlier word of encouragement along the Way:

"Fear not, little flock, it is your Father's good pleasure to give you the Kingdom."

[EXIT PORTAL: TWO PARABLES ON PRAYER]

• And he spake a parable unto them to the end that they ought always to pray, and not to faint; saying, There was in a city a judge, who feared not God, and regarded not man: and there was a widow in that city; and she came oft unto him, saying, Avenge me of mine adversary. And he would not for a while: but afterward he said within himself, Though I fear not God, nor regard man; yet because this widow troubleth me, I will avenge her, lest she wear me out by her continual coming. And the Lord said, Hear what the unrighteous judge saith. And shall not God avenge his elect, that cry to him day and night, and [yet] he is longsuffering over them? I say unto you, that he will avenge them speedily. Nevertheless, when the Son of man cometh, shall he find faith on the earth?

• And he spake also this parable unto certain who trusted in themselves that they were righteous, and set all others at nought. Two men went up into the Temple to pray; the one a Pharisee, and the other a publican. The Pharisee stood and prayed thus with himself, God, I thank thee, that I am not as the rest of men, extortioners, unjust, adulterers, or even as this publican. I fast twice in the week; I give tithes of all that I get. But the publican, standing afar off, would not lift up so much as his eyes unto heaven, but smote his breast, saying, God, be thou merciful to me, a sinner. I say unto you, This man went down to his house justified rather than the other, for every one that exalteth himself shall be humbled; but he that humbleth himself shall be exalted.

———·•·———

Reflections

Despite the seriousness of the subject, the Sermon is almost childlike. It rarely quotes the grownup Scriptures. It teaches mostly by stories, helping the beginner visualize the lesson. The final pair of exit pieces, like the then popular Aesop fables, first say what they are going to be about, and at the end, repeat the lesson. In the Sermon as a whole, Luke the Physician gives the prognosis, and he gives it straight: Discipleship is not for everyone; it needs commitment. It may bring persecution, and those who later renounce it forfeit eternal life. But at the ends of sections, Luke now and then scatters encouragements.

The Christian Way is a Way of Prayer, Luke tells us at the end. And prayer will be heard; the prayers of the humble will *assuredly* be heard. Those who are humble (and none more than a child) shall in the end be exalted. Luke at the end of his Sermon looks forward to the successful end of the individual life.

38. Restoring the Law
Matthew 23:1-3a

Luke A had taken Mark's Jesus further in the renunciation direction: believers must sacrifice every worldly advantage for their Heavenly reward. Matthew, coming shortly after, takes a contrary approach. Jesus, following the later prophets, had reduced the Law to six clauses: our relations with others. Returning instead to the older Scriptures, Matthew reinstates the whole Law.[1] He even affirms the authority of Jesus' opponents, the scribes and Pharisees, as being the correct interpreters of the Law. Or so it seems at first:

Then spake Jesus to the multitudes and to his disciples, saying, The scribes and the Pharisees sit on Moses' seat; all things therefore whatsoever they bid you, do and observe . . .

———————··•··———————

[1]Matthew 5:17-18, "Think not that I came to destroy the law or the prophets; I came not to destroy, but to fulfil. For verily I say unto you, Till heaven and earth pass away, one jot or one tittle shall in nowise pass away from the law till all things be accomplished." The contradiction with Jesus does not matter; Matthew has his strategy.

Reflections

Having reinstated the Scriptures, Matthew then takes possession of them, by asserting that they are fulfilled in Jesus. The fulfilment of Scripture in Jesus had previously been asserted just once, in Mark. That was at the Arrest:

Mk 14:49. I was daily with you in the Temple teaching, and ye took me not; but let the Scriptures be fulfilled.

Matthew preserves this passage more or less intact, and adds ten fulfillments of his own, each marked by a recurring final formula. The ten formulas are:

- Mt 1:22-23 [Birth of Jesus] . . . that it might be fulfilled which was spoken by the Lord through the prophet, saying [q Isaiah 7:15]
- Mt 2:15 [Departure for Egypt] . . . that it might be fulfilled which was spoken by the Lord through the prophet, saying [q Hosea 11:1]
- Mt 2:17-18 [Slaying of the Infants]. Then was fulfilled that which was spoken through Jeremiah the prophet, saying [q Jer 31:15]
- Mt 2:23 [Dwelling in Nazareth] . . . that it might be fulfilled which was spoken through the prophets, that he should be called a Nazarene [very contorted echo of Judges 13:7, "for the child shall be a Nazirite"]
- Mt 4:14-16 [Dwelling in Capernaum] . . . that it might be fulfilled which was spoken through Isaiah the prophet, saying [q Isaiah 8:23–9:1]
- Mt 8:17 [Healing in Capernaum] . . . that it might be fulfilled which was spoken through Isaiah the prophet, saying [q Isaiah 53:4].
- Mt 12:17-21 [Healings following the Sabbath healing of the Man with the Withered Hand] . . . that it might be fulfilled which was spoken through Isaiah the prophet, saying [q Isaiah 42:1-4]
- Mt 13:35 [end of the Kingdom parables] . . . that it might be fulfilled which was spoken through the prophet, saying [q Psalm 29:30]
- Mt 21:4-5 [Jesus riding into Jerusalem] . . . that it might be fulfilled which was spoken through the prophet, saying [q Zechariah 9:9]
- Mt 27:9-10 [Returning the pieces of silver] . . .[q Zechariah 11:13b]

Matthew was the first to include a Birth Narrative, and four of his fulfillments support that new material. Most of the others support other Matthean novelties (where Jesus lived, what he rode into Jerusalem). What is the point of this? Part of it is to back up Matthew's innovations against the earlier Mark and Luke. But the main idea is to show that in all details, Jesus is foretold by Scripture. If even here, how much more in claims like that made by the heavenly voice at the baptism (Mt 3:17, "This is my beloved Son, in whom I am well pleased")? Scripture is the final authority. The right to interpret Scripture is accordingly the highest power in Judaism.

Who has that power? *Who owns Judaism?*

Matthew answers that question in part by his denunciation of the Pharisees.

39. Woes Unto the Pharisees
Matthew 23

*Matthew makes Jesus restore all the Law: "Think not that I came to destroy
the Law or the Prophets: I came not to destroy but to fulfil. For verily, I say
unto you, Till heaven and earth pass away, one jot or one tittle shall in no wise
pass away from the Law, till all things be accomplished" (5:17-18). Matthew
seems to accept the Pharisees as interpreters of the Law, but he has no good
word to say of them as examples of lawfulness. At the end, he extends his
disapproval to all Jerusalem, and to all Jews. What is going on here?*

Then spake Jesus to the multitudes and to his disciples, saying, The scribes
and the Pharisees sit on Moses' seat; all things therefore whatsoever they bid
you, do and observe. But do not ye after their works; for they say, and do not.
Yea, they bind heavy burdens and grievous to be borne, and lay them on men's
shoulders; but they themselves will not move them with their finger. But all
their works they do to be seen of men: for they make broad their phylacteries,
and enlarge the borders [of their garments], and love the chief place at feasts,
and the chief seats in the synagogues, and the salutations in the marketplaces,
and to be called of men, Rabbi.

But be not ye called Rabbi: for one is your teacher, and all ye are brethren.
And call no man your father on the earth, for one is your Father: he who is in
heaven. Neither be ye called masters, for one is your master: the Christ. But he
that is greatest among you shall be your servant. And whosoever shall exalt
himself shall be humbled; and whosoever shall humble himself shall be exalted.

But woe unto you, scribes and Pharisees, hypocrites! Because ye shut the
kingdom of heaven against men: for ye enter not in yourselves, neither suffer
ye them that are entering in to enter.

Woe unto you, scribes and Pharisees, hypocrites! For ye compass sea and
land to make one proselyte; and when he is become so, ye make him twofold
more a son of hell than yourselves.

Woe unto you, ye blind guides, that say, Whosoever shall swear by the
temple, it is nothing; but whosoever shall swear by the gold of the temple, he
is a debtor. Ye fools and blind: for which is greater, the gold, or the temple that
hath sanctified the gold?

And, Whosoever shall swear by the altar, it is nothing; but whosoever shall
swear by the gift that is upon it, he is a debtor. Ye blind: for which is greater,
the gift, or the altar that sanctifieth the gift? He therefore that sweareth by the
altar, sweareth by it, and by all things thereon. And he that sweareth by the
temple, sweareth by it, and by him that dwelleth therein. And he that sweareth
by the heaven, sweareth by the throne of God, and by him that sitteth thereon

Woe unto you, scribes and Pharisees, hypocrites! For ye tithe mint and anise and cummin, and have left undone the weightier matters of the law, justice, and mercy, and faith: but these ye ought to have done, and not to have left the other undone. Ye blind guides, that strain out the gnat, and swallow the camel!

Woe unto you, scribes and Pharisees, hypocrites! For ye cleanse the outside of the cup and of the platter, but within they are full from extortion and excess. Thou blind Pharisee, cleanse first the inside of the cup and of the platter, that the outside thereof may become clean also.

Woe unto you, scribes and Pharisees, hypocrites! For ye are like unto whited sepulchres, which outwardly appear beautiful, but inwardly are full of dead men's bones, and of all uncleanness. Even so ye also outwardly appear righteous unto men, but inwardly ye are full of hypocrisy and iniquity.

Woe unto you, scribes and Pharisees, hypocrites! For ye build the sepulchres of the prophets, and garnish the tombs of the righteous, and say, If we had been in the days of our fathers, we should not have been partakers with them in the blood of the prophets. Wherefore ye witness to yourselves, that ye are sons of them that slew the prophets. Fill ye up then the measure of your fathers. Ye serpents, ye offspring of vipers, how shall ye escape the judgment of hell? Therefore, behold, I send unto you prophets, and wise men, and scribes: some of them shall ye kill and crucify; and some of them shall ye scourge in your synagogues, and persecute from city to city: that upon you may come all the righteous blood shed on the earth, from the blood of Abel the righteous unto the blood of Zachariah son of Barachiah, whom ye slew between the sanctuary and the altar. Verily I say unto you, all these things shall come upon this generation.

O Jerusalem, Jerusalem, that killeth the prophets, and stoneth them that are sent unto her! How often would I have gathered thy children together, even as a hen gathereth her chickens under her wings, and ye would not! Behold, your house is left unto you desolate. For I say unto you, Ye shall not see me henceforth, till ye shall say, Blessed [is] he that cometh in the name of the Lord.

------- ••••• -------

Reflections

Jesus had challenged the Rabbinic system as intrinsically flawed. Matthew keeps all the Law and the Prophets, but interprets them as speaking of Christ. He reinstates, and then appropriates, the Scriptures. His nominal acceptance of the Pharisees is canceled by his rejection of their example. He has Jesus *replace* them in the system. Again the challenge: *Who owns Judaism?*

Meanwhile, with the destruction of the Temple, its sacrificial center, in 70, Judaism had its own problems. Not who owned it, but would it survive at all?

Crisis

40. Yoḥanan ben Zakkai
Mishnah: Rosh Hasshanah 4

Judaism had always been a religion of sacrifice. After Solomon built the first Temple and centralized the sacrifices in his capital Jerusalem, it had been a religion of sacrifice at the Jerusalem Temple. When the Romans put down the Jewish Revolt of 68-72, they destroyed the Temple. Learned rabbis, some of the Sadducee and some of the Pharisee party, gathered at Yabneh, west of Jerusalem, and considered what to do. This was Judaism's moment of decision: what kind of religion would it now be? The answer was to keep the sacrificial observances in place, but to diffuse them: to the towns with a Rabbinic court, and to the local synagogues.

The great figure in this transition was Yohanan ben Zakkai, whose rulings on how the old observances shall be continued (or in some cases abandoned) are preserved in the Mishnah, the earliest compilation of Rabbinic traditions. Here are four of Yohanan's decisions about ritual continuation.

The festival day of the New Year which coincided with the Sabbath: in the Temple they would sound the shofar, but not in the provinces. When the Temple was destroyed, Rabban Yoḥanan ben Zakkai made the rule that they should sound the shofar in every locale in which there was a court. (4:1)

[Formerly], the lulab was taken up in the Temple for seven days, and in the provinces, for one day. When the Temple was destroyed, Rabban Yoḥanan ben Zakkai made the rule that in the provinces the lulab should be taken up for seven days, as a memorial to the Temple; and that the day on which the omer is waved [16th Nisan] should be wholly prohibited [in regard to the eating of new produce]. (4:3)

At first they would receive testimony about the new moon[1] all day long. One time witnesses came late, and the Levites . . . made the rule that they should receive testimony only up to the afternoon offering . . . When the Temple was destroyed, Rabban Yoḥanan ben Zakkai made the rule that they should [once more] receive testimony about the new moon all day long. (4:4)

Said R Joshua ben Qorha, This rule too did Rabban Yoḥanan ben Zakkai make: Even if the head of the court is located somewhere else, the witnesses should come only to the location of the council [to give testimony, and not to the location of the head of the court]. (4:4)

---

[1]The date of the festival was fixed by direct observation of the new moon.

Reflections

Yoḥanan was first known as a judge at the local court in the Galilee town of Gabara.[2] Two of his Sabbath rulings from that early period are preserved:

[On the Sabbath] they cover a lamp with a dish, so that it will not scorch a rafter, and the excrement of a child, and a scorpion, so that it will not bite. Said R Judah, A case came before Rabban Yoḥanan ben Zakkai in Arab, and he said, I suspect [he is liable] for a sin offering. (Shabbat 16:7)

[On the Sabbath] someone breaks a jar to eat dried figs from it . . . Said R Judah, A case came before Rabban Yoḥanan ben Zakkai in Arab, and he said, I fear on his account that he should bring a sin offering [for violating the Sabbath]. (Shabbat 22:3)

His origins were modest, and his early rulings were notably strict. His teacher was probably his father, Zakkai or Zacchaeus. What happened at Yabneh under his leadership was the establishment of a control center to replace Jerusalem, a center from which rulings could be passed down to the court towns and the local synagogues.

Thus, at the moment of their decision, did the rabbis abandon the Prophets, the ethical tendency which Jesus and his later movement had been developing, and choose instead the Law. The basis for the final separation had been laid.

The new network of local courts and still more local synagogues which the rabbis defined was not unlike the old Christian system of Apostolic control, exerted from centers in Capernaum and Jerusalem, by personal visits and by circular letters, which had come to an end with the deaths of the chief Apostles only a few years earlier. The Christian response to the loss of *their* centralized system was to strengthen local churches and to provide new text authorities. There was no one figure comparable to Yoḥanan. That role was taken by three: Luke, who updated the old Gospel of Mark to give guidance for new questions; Matthew, who produced a quite different replacement for Mark, in which he challenged the rabbis on their central ground of the Law; and on the Paul side, a committee under Onesimus, which edited Paul's letters for wider circulation, and went on to issue new letters under Paul's name, stating the qualifications for the new church leaders. Paul's followers took such positions themselves: the former slave Onesimus went on to become the Bishop of Ephesus.

And as one aspect of getting their act own together again, the Jesus people sought to patch up the quarrel between their Alpha and Beta factions.

---

[2]Gabara (Hebrew "Arab"), in central Galilee, was one of the towns which supplied priests for the Temple. It was destroyed by Vespasian in 66, during the Jewish War.

41. Including Alpha
Romans 1:18-32, abridged

Paul in Romans had taken a hard line against the Alphas. The Alphas, in response, in the last addition to Jacob of Alphaeus' church letter, had ridiculed Paul's Abraham theory. Paul's editors, around the year 71, coming to the task of presenting Paul to future generations, were concerned not only to generalize Paul's advice to specific churches, but to damp down all such controversies. They did this for the Alpha/Beta conflict by inserting passages which seemed to preach Alpha doctrines, so that the Alphas too could regard Paul as speaking to their condition, and happily go forward, under Paul's leadership, into the shared Christian future.

Part of the Alpha heritage from Judaism was the Atonement Prayer, a list of sins for which one asks forgiveness. One version of this list was added to Galatians (at 5:13-6:10, where it interrupts a diatribe against circumcision). Another was inserted in Romans. Here are the beginning and the end of it:

For the wrath of God is revealed from heaven against all ungodliness and unrighteousness of men, who hinder the truth in unrighteousness; because that which is known of God is manifest in them; for God manifested it unto them. For the invisible things of him since the creation of the world are clearly seen, being perceived through the things that are made, [even] his everlasting power and divinity; that they may be without excuse: because that, knowing God, they glorified him not as God, neither gave thanks; but became vain in their reasonings, and their senseless heart was darkened . . . Wherefore God gave them up in the lusts of their hearts unto uncleanness, that their bodies should be dishonored among themselves: for that they exchanged the truth of God for a lie, and worshiped and served the creature rather than the Creator, who is blessed for ever. Amen . . .

And even as they refused to have God in [their] knowledge, God gave them up unto a reprobate mind, to do those things which are not fitting; being filled with all unrighteousness, wickedness, covetousness, maliciousness; full of envy, murder, strife, deceit, malignity; whisperers, backbiters, hateful to God, insolent, haughty, boastful, inventors of evil things, disobedient to parents, without understanding, covenant-breakers, without natural affection, unmerciful: who, knowing the ordinance of God, that they that practice such things are worthy of death, not only do the same, but also consent with them that practice them.

Reflections

That last paragraph brings in the Atonement prayer. Each of the 22 items in the original Hebrew of that prayer began with a different letter of the Hebrew alphabet; they were recited in alphabetical order.[1] As preserved in the Didache (which is in Greek, and thus does not display the alphabetical order), they were:

1. murders φόνοι
2. adulteries μοιχεῖαι
3. lusts ἐπιθυμίαι
4. fornications πορνεῖαι
5. thefts κλοπαί
6. idolatries εἰδωλολατρίαι
7. feats of magic μαγεῖαι
8. sorceries φαρμακίαι
9. robberies ἁρπαγαί
10. false witness ψευδομαρτυρίαι
11. hypocrisies ὑποκρίσεις
12. double-heartedness διπλοκαρδία
13. deceit δόλος
14. pride ὑπερηφανία
15. malice κακία
16. willfulness αὐθάδεια
17. coveting πλεονεξία
18. foul speech αἰσχρολογία
19. jealousy ζηλοτυπία
20. audacity θρασύτης
21. hauteur ὕψος
22. boastfulness ἀλαζονεία

It is an interesting project to match these terms against the Romans list. What did the editors think it well to change, forty years after Jesus had died, leaving behind followers who still taught, and practiced, that prayer?

In various ways, the editors, and Paul's successors in general, sought to end the war between Alpha and Beta theologies. They gave the Atonement less prominence than Paul had done (he had radically opposed the Alpha theory, that one's deeds were important for one's salvation). The Beta idea was there, in these later "Pauline" texts, but so was Alpha, and the Atonement theory was thus less insistent than it had been in Paul's original letter.

And sometimes, in later writings in the Gospel tradition, the Atonement idea was not there at all.

---

[1] For details, see Brooks **Two Ways**, which includes an analysis of this passage.

42. Preaching at Athens
Acts 17:22-34

The doctrine of the Atonement (that Jesus' death alone saves all from sin), was probably a Jerusalem concept, since it is based on the theory of sacrifice. In Mark, written in Jerusalem, it appears in Mk 10:45 and 14:24, two late passages, and so was not an original Christian doctrine. Luke hated that idea. He did not copy it from Mark (the corresponding Lk 12:27 and 22:26 lack it), and when he later came in Acts II to add the story of Paul to his original Acts, he never shows Paul as preaching that doctrine. Luke felt that the approach to the Gentiles had to be on a different basis, the one Paul himself uses in Romans when addressing Gentiles – the concept of the Creator God in nature.

With a certain amount of implied humor, Luke imagines Paul as preaching to Gentiles in Athens, and doing so on those terms – but losing his audience when he mentions Jesus' miraculous Resurrection. The Areopagus was a forum in Athens, on a high place where philosophical disputations were often held.

And Paul stood in the midst of the Areopagus, and said, Ye men of Athens, in all things I perceive that ye are very religious. For as I passed along, and observed the objects of your worship, I found also an altar with this inscription: TO AN UNKNOWN GOD. What therefore ye worship in ignorance, this I set forth unto you.

The God that made the world and all things therein, he, being Lord of heaven and earth, dwelleth not in temples made with hands, neither is he served by men's hands, as though he needed anything, seeing he himself giveth to us all life, and breath, and all things; and he made of every nation of men to dwell on all the face of the earth, having determined their appointed seasons, and the bounds of their habitation, that they should seek God, if haply they might feel after him and find him, though he is not far from each one of us, for in him we live and move, and have our being, as certain even of your own poets have said.

For we are also his offspring.

Being then the offspring of God, we ought not to think that the Godhead is like unto gold, or silver, or stone, graven by art and device of man. The times of ignorance therefore God overlooked, but now he commandeth men that they should all everywhere repent, inasmuch as he hath appointed a day in which he will judge the world in righteousness, by the man whom he hath ordained, whereof he hath given assurance unto all men, in that he raised him from the dead.

———————··•··———————

Reflections

Gentiles, and perhaps especially the philosophically inclined Athenians, could not be effectively approached by talking of Abraham's sacrifice of Isaac, as Paul does in Romans, or by basing the appeal on anything else accepted by the Jews but unknown or without authority elsewhere. The approach must be universal. In Romans, or one part of it addressed to Gentiles, Paul had argued:

> For as many as have sinned without the Law shall also perish without the Law, and as many as have sinned under the Law shall be judged by the Law, for not the hearers of the Law who are just before God, but the doers of the Law shall be justified. (For when Gentiles that have not the Law do by nature the things of the Law, these, not having the Law, are the Law unto themselves, in that they the work of the Law written in their hearts, their conscience bearing witness therewith, and their thoughts one with another accusing or else excusing), in the day when God shall judge the secrets of men, according to my Gospel, by Christ Jesus. (Rom 2:12-16)

Luke in his invented Areopagus speech has Paul begin that way, gaining his audience's assent and recognition by quoting a well-known Greek poet, Aratus.

Then, as Luke imagines it, and as Paul had in the above Romans passage, Paul goes on to annex, to this astronomical and theological grandeur, a claimed miraculous resurrection of a Jewish rebel of whom the Athenians would not have heard, or if they had heard, had heard in unfavorable terms. He bombs out, and the scene ends. The result in terms of converts is paltry:

> Now when they heard of the resurrection of the dead, some mocked, but others said, We will hear thee concerning this yet again. Thus Paul went out from among them. But certain men clave unto him, and believed, among whom was also Dionysius the Areopagite and a woman named Damaris, and others with them. (Acts 17:32-34)

Which (so Luke invites us to infer) is why Paul founded no church in Athens.

Thus did Luke, himself a post-Pauline writer, join forces with some of Paul's own later editors, who in preparing his letters for wider circulation, tended to omit, or to include only in the mildest and the most perfunctory terms, the controversial doctrine of the Atonement.

There were other points of Paul's teaching, or the practice of his churches, which the editors felt needed adjustment; in one case to conform Christian practice to the customs of the Roman Empire, including those of most Jews. That point concerned the social role and public visibility of women.

43. The Question of Women
1 Corinthians 11:2-16

Paul's letters were edited by his associates, around 71. One thing they did, as we have just seen, was to minimize the conflict between Paul and the Alpha Christians. Another area of conflict was women. In Paul's churches, women sometimes held positions of leadership, in contrast to their sharply limited social role outside. This led to tensions with the outside world, which the editors were concerned to cool down. Passages were added to Paul's letters which prescribed female conduct more in line with conventional ideas.

One such passage is this one, which was interpolated into 1 Corinthians. The verses before and after it are included, to make the interpolation obvious:

Now I praise you that ye remember me in all things, and hold fast the traditions, even as I delivered them to you.

But I would have you know that the head of every man is Christ, the head of the woman is the man, and the head of Christ is God. Any man praying or prophesying, having his head covered, dishonoreth his head. But every woman praying or prophesying with her head unveiled dishonoreth her head, for it is one and the same thing as if she were shaven. For if a woman is not veiled, let her also be shorn, but if it is a shame to a woman to be shorn or shaven, let her be veiled. For a man indeed ought not to have his head veiled, forasmuch as he is the image and glory of God, but the woman is the glory of the man. For the man is not of the woman, but the woman of the man, for neither was the man created for the woman, but the woman for the man. For this cause ought the woman to have a sign of authority on her head,because of angels. Nevertheless, neither is the woman without the man, nor the man without the woman, in the Lord. For as the woman is of the man, so is the man also by the woman, but all things are of God. Judge ye in yourselves: Is it seemly that a woman pray unto God unveiled? Doth not even nature itself teach you, that if a man have long hair, it is a dishonor to him, but if a woman have long hair, it is a a glory to her, for her hair is given her for a covering. But if any man seemeth to be contentious, we have no such custom, neither do the churches of God.

But in giving you this charge, I praise you not . . .

───────··•··───────

Reflections

Three things give this passage away as an interpolation. One, it is off topic; the announced subject of this part of 1 Corinthians is food offered to idols, and communal food in general, not hair. Two, it is interruptive. The passages before and after it are on the subject of food, and the word "praise" in the verse before this passage is picked up by the refusal to "praise" in the verse following. Removing our passage joins them together again. Three, notice "neither the churches of God." It was the main purpose of Paul's editors to make his highly specific church letters seem to have universal application, and this phrase, which implies all churches, not just Corinth, helps to accomplish that.

Recognizing the interpolation is merely a technical matter. Its importance for us is that it lets us see behind the text in our Bibles, to detect what of Paul's letter is really Paul's, and what later additions now jostle it, confusing our sense of what Paul himself was really like, and really said.

What it comes to is that female followers of Jesus should appear modestly, as the outside world is accustomed to judge modesty; and appropriately, as that world defines appropriateness. It does not limit membership, or forbid women to prophesy. It does present a more conventional face to the outside world.

This is not the only passage about the role of women. A few, like this one, were added to Paul's letters. Others figure in the letters written after Paul, and claiming his authority, but actually written by Paul's associates.[1]

The theological compromise, the "both-and" stance which Paul's editors created toward Alpha and Beta in these additions to Pauline tradition, held for only a little while; that compromise would later come apart. The diminution of the role of women caused no such rupture; it seems to have been accepted in the mainstream (though texts featuring women as major figures did appear in the popular tradition).

Of more concern in the mainstream tradition was the challenge of theories offering a different, and more magical, account of salvation itself.

---

[1] For detailed help in identifying them, see Collins **Letters**.

44. The Fullness of God
Colossians 1:13-20

Colossians, supposedly written by Paul to Colossae, is actually by Paul's manager, Onesimus; it introduces the collection of Paul's letters which was edited under his supervision. Speaking for Paul, he takes Paul's theology a little further. In this hymn, he goes beyond the idea that Jesus by his death reconciles men to God, and that by his resurrection he assures believers' ascent to Heaven. He goes beyond the heavenly origin of Jesus which was asserted in the Philippi hymn; he now makes Jesus indistinguishable from God: the creator not only of the world, of all things in their fullness (the pleroma), but of institutions, both heavenly and earthly. The institution which Onesimus, the future Bishop of Ephesus, has most in mind is the church: an institution of which Christ is the head, directing its doings. By being members of the church, believers are already identified with this larger universe.

13[1] He who delivered us from the power of darkness
     and transferred us into the Kingdom of the Son of his love,
14 in whom we have redemption, the forgiveness of our sins.
15   For he is the image of the invisible God,
       First-born before all created things,
16   For in him were all things created
       in heaven and on earth,
       visible and invisible,
       Thrones or Princes,
       Powers or Authorities,

All have been created through him and for him.
17 And he is before all things,
     and all things subsist in him.
18   And he is the head of the body, the church,
       he the beginning, the first-born from the dead,
       that in all things he might have the primacy,
19   for in him by God's own will the fullness of God dwelt,
20   and through him God reconciled all things,
       made peace on his account through the blood of his cross,
       peace through him on earth as in heaven.

———————————·••·•——————————

[1]Most commentators work only with 1:15-20; Vielhauer has seen that 1:13-14 must also be included, in order to give a symmetrical two-stanza form for Colossians.

Reflections

There it is, the universe. The sun and the moon, the stars in their courses, the seasons in their sequence, night and day in succession, the myriad things (wàn-wù 萬物) of which the classical Chinese philosophers speak – does it have anything to do with us? So some had thought, and not only in China: the Pythagoreans had included all of Nature in their world system. In earlier times, Jews too had been impressed by the regularities of nature, and seen divinities as residing in the stars, helping to determine the fates of men.

It is these ideas which are typical of what is usually called Gnosticism, and the allusions to them in the Colossians hymn have led some to suppose that the Colossians hymn has a Gnostic hymn as its original. More likely, Onesimus is simply adorning his own beliefs with these details from the nature philosophers, to give them greater reach and dignity.

Paul himself had gone a fair distance toward an esoteric understanding of salvation, in a passage rejected by some as Gnostic:

> We speak Wisdom (Σοφίαν), however, among them that are fullgrown, yet a wisdom not of this world, nor of the rulers of this world, who are coming to nought; but we speak God's wisdom in a mystery, even the wisdom that hath been hidden, which God foreordained before the worlds unto our glory, which none of the rulers of this world hath known . . . but unto us God revealed them, through the spirit, for the Spirit teacheth all things, yea, the deep things of God. (1 Corinthians 2:6-8, 10).

For Paul, what was central was a mystical unity with Christ; he saw baptism as participating in the death of Christ: being bathed in his blood. What was passionate and individual in Paul becomes orderly and general in Onesimus, who even in Colossians emphasizes right behavior, not at odds with right faith (as we have seen it was for Paul), but as *compatible* with faith.

Against other features of the Gnosticism of his time, Onesimus held firm.

45. Principalities and Powers
Colossians 2:8-15

Lest some Gnostically-inclined readers should be encouraged by his hymn, Onesimus takes care, in the next chapter, to distance himself (and also them) from dangerous aspects of contemporary thought, whether Gnostic or Jewish. In all this post-Pauline literature, "philosophy" is a negative term.

Take heed lest there shall be any one that maketh spoil of you through his philosophy and vain deceit, alter the tradition of men after the rudiments of the world[1] and not after Christ, for in him dwelleth all the fullness of the Godhead bodily, and in him are ye made full, who is the head of all principality and power; in whom ye were also circumcised with a circumcision not made with hands, in the putting off of the body of the flesh, in the circumcision of Christ; having been buried with him in baptism, wherein ye were also raised with him through faith in the working of God, who raised him from the dead.

And you, being dead through your trespasses and the uncircumcision of your flesh, you, I say, did he make alive together with him, having forgiven us all our trespasses; having blotted out the bond written in ordinances that was against us, which was contrary to us; and he hath taken it out of the way, nailing it to the cross; having despoiled the principalities and the powers, he made a show of them openly, triumphing over them in it.

---

[1] The "elemental spirits of the cosmos" (στοιχεῖα τοῦ κοσμόυ): not earthly regimes but supernatural powers as part of the universe.

Reflections

On one level, this asserts the power of Christ over the rulers of this world, the Romans and their Jewish accomplices who seemed to have killed him, but whom he has refuted and disgraced by his Resurrection. And also over Jewish conventions about circumcision and the whole extent of the Law, which would condemn them, but the list of our sins is canceled by his sacrifice on the Cross. But "principalities and powers" also has in mind the rulers ("archons") who in one Jewish Gnostic view inhabit the stars, and oppose the ascent of the soul, returning to its heavenly home.

These ideas were popular, as we can see from the many attempts to refute them. Here is a prayer of the returning soul, attempting to get past one archon, as quoted in Origen's tract Against Celsus:[2]

> When they have passed through Ialdabaoth and have come to Iao, they are to say, "You second Archon of the hidden mysteries of Son and Father, night-shining Iao, first master of Death, part of the blameless, bearing your beard as a symbol: I am ready to pass by your rule. By the living word I have overpowered him who came from you. Let Grace be with me, Father, let it be with me."

The final sentence is addressed not to evil Iao, but to the good God high above.

In Onesimus' view, the pleroma (the Fullness of nature) in the Gnostic system is replaced by the Fullness of Christ, in whom all of nature subsists. That Fullness of Christ is embodied in the Church, through which members partake in it. Salvation is by Christ, and access to Christ is through the Church. This is not Gnosticism, instead, it is a functional replacement for the Gnostic vision of the cosmos.

As a mere literary aside, we may notice the very heavy style of Colossians. Sentences may run on for a whole paragraph. This is a weariness for the reader, but it is a joy for the orator, who will emphasize each phrase in turn, letting it resonate in the ears of his hearers before going on to the next. It is not so much a sentence as a string of phrases, each one asserting some major tenet of faith. Colossians is less a written document than a script for preaching.

Literarily, then, Onesimus was more than ready to take on a preaching job. So were not a few others, as the Pastoral Epistles in particular bear witness.

---

[2]Translation adapted from Grant **Gnosticism** 91.

46. The Bishops
Titus 1:5-11 and 2:1-15

The post-Apostolic vacuum gave more power to the leaders of the newly independent churches. What qualities should they have? How are they chosen? To this practical question, and to a few others, such as the need to be at peace with secular society, the Pastoral Epistles addressed themselves. These are three compositions by Paul's associates but put out under his name to give their prescriptions his sanction.[1] One of these was by Titus. He depicts Paul as addressing him – and incidentally, as giving him full authority in Crete:

For this cause left I thee in Crete, that thou shouldest set in order the things that were wanting, and appoint elders in every city, as I gave thee charge; if any man is blameless, the husband of one wife, having children that believe, who are not accused of riot or unruly. For the bishop must be blameless, as God's steward; not self-willed, not soon angry, no brawler, no striker, not greedy of filthy lucre; but given to hospitality, a lover of good, sober-minded, just, holy, self-controlled; holding to the faithful word which is according to the teaching, that he may be able to exhort in the sound doctrine, and to convict the gainsayers. For there are many unruly men, vain talkers and deceivers, specially they of the circumcision, whose mouths must be stopped; men who overthrow whole houses, teaching things which they ought not, for filthy lucre's sake.

But speak thou the things which befit the sound doctrine: that aged men be temperate, grave, sober-minded, sound in faith, in love, in patience: that aged women likewise be reverent in demeanor, not slanderers nor enslaved to much wine, teachers of that which is good; that they may train the young women to love their husbands, to love their children, [to be] sober-minded, chaste, workers at home, kind, being in subjection to their own husbands, that the word of God be not blasphemed: the younger men likewise exhort to be sober-minded: in all things showing thyself an example of good works; in thy doctrine [showing] uncorruptness, gravity, sound speech, that cannot be condemned; that he that is of the contrary part may be ashamed, having no evil thing to say of us. [Exhort] servants to be in subjection to their own masters, [and] to be well-pleasing [to them] in all things; not gainsaying; not purloining, but showing all good fidelity; that they may adorn the doctrine of God our Saviour in all things.

---·•••·---

[1]See Easton **Pastoral**, and for the spurious epistles generally, Collins **Letters**.

Reflections

"Paul" here establishes qualifications for Bishops, while in effect giving Titus that authority in the substantial territory of Crete. Chances are that Titus himself has composed what amounts to a letter of appointment.

The requirements for office are worth a moment's notice. They are mostly personal, and the personal ones are on the mild side. It would be difficult to fit vehement Paul into that pattern, and we may have here a self-portrait of Titus. As to doctrine, the bishop should be firm. The accusation that those who think otherwise do it for money is an insult typical of the Paul school. We notice that doctrine itself *is a fully known quantity.* Any divergence, any discussion at all, is to be treated harshly. This trend characterizes the Jesus movement after 70. It was defining itself more precisely. It was hardening up.

In the second of the above extracts, the author turns again to doctrine, and again the substance is mostly personal: sobriety, submissiveness, good sense. That outsiders should have nothing evil to say of the Christians was a note already struck in the editorial interpolations in Paul's letters, and continues at full strength here. It would be easy to imagine Titus as among Paul's editors, making similar adjustments in Paul's own letters.

We may note in passing the rule that slaves should not "purloin." Onesimus had gotten into trouble with his master by doing something of that kind. Is this possibly a dig at Onesimus, whose leadership among Paul's editors, and whose later position at Ephesus, Titus might have resented?

We are now approaching the crisis of our story. As preparation, we may look in on an unknown pastor, not of the Paul party but of that persuasion theologically. He is distributing to the churches in his area a sermon preached to those just baptized. The author knows the Epistle of Jacob, the circular letter which seems to have reached every church of which we have record, and he borrows a phrase or two from that. The Christian way was one of hardship and danger, and of those dangers he duly warns the newly baptized.

47. A Baptismal Homily
1 Peter 1:3 – 4:13

Here is a sermon preached to those entering on the Christian life. We do not know the author's name, but he was probably a person of authority in north Asia Minor, perhaps at the great Black Sea port of Sinope. One thing of which we can be confident: he was not Peter (though a few years later, that name would be attached to the text). Nor was he an Alpha Christian; he preaches a Beta view of the saving death of Jesus.

The Homily starts, naturally enough, with baptism itself: the moment when one formally becomes a Christian. It says what Baptism is, and how it derives not from some recent innovation of John the Baptist, but on the contrary (in the theological style of this part of the second half of the 1st century), goes back to the beginning of the world. It is only the revelation of that long hidden mystery that belongs to the present age. To those just baptized, these ancient mysteries have at last been revealed.

This is a long chapter, and this Introduction has therefore been distributed over the several sections of the text, to highlight its structure, and to provide a more helpful running commentary.

Blessed [be] the God and Father of our Lord Jesus Christ, who according to his great mercy begat us again unto a living hope by the resurrection of Jesus Christ from the dead, unto an inheritance incorruptible, and undefiled, and that fadeth not away, reserved in heaven for you, who by the power of God are guarded through faith unto a salvation ready to be revealed in the last time. Wherein ye greatly rejoice, though now for a little while, if need be, ye have been put to grief in manifold trials, that the proof of your faith, [being] more precious than gold that perisheth though it is proved by fire, may be found unto praise and glory and honor at the revelation of Jesus Christ, whom not having seen ye love; on whom, though now ye see him not, yet believing, ye rejoice greatly with joy unspeakable and full of glory, receiving the end of your faith, [even] the salvation of [your] souls.

Concerning which salvation the prophets sought and searched diligently, who prophesied of the grace that [should come] unto you: searching what [time] or what manner of time the Spirit of Christ which was in them did point unto, when it testified beforehand the sufferings of Christ, and the glories that should follow them. To whom it was revealed, that not unto themselves, but unto you, did they minister these things, which now have been announced unto you through them that preached the gospel unto you by the Holy Spirit sent forth from heaven; which things angel desire to look into.

Now we come to the proper behavior of one who is admitted to these secrets, which not even the angels know: to be sinless. To be sinless is to be close to God; indeed, to be like God. It is not only Jesus, but now also we, the believers in Jesus, who are become Sons of God. And over us God will watch, as a father over his sons.

Wherefore girding up the loins of your mind, be sober and set your hope perfectly on the grace that is to be brought unto you at the revelation of Jesus Christ, as children of obedience, not fashioning yourselves according to your former lusts in [the time of] your ignorance, but like as he who called you is holy, be ye yourselves also holy in all manner of living. Because it is written, Ye shall be holy; for I am holy. And if ye call on him as Father, who without respect of persons judgeth according to each man's work, pass the time of your sojourning in fear, knowing that ye were redeemed, not with corruptible things, with silver or gold, from your vain manner of life handed down from your fathers; but with precious blood, as of a lamb without spot, of Christ, who was foreknown indeed before the foundation of the world, but was manifested at the end of times for your sake, who through him are believers in God, that raised him from the dead, and gave him glory; so that your faith and hope might be in God.

Next, the sermon takes up the love of the brethren, the need to forsake all worldly aspirations, and to live entirely within the Community of the Saved. Everything else (and here we have an echo of the Epistle of Jacob), however lovely in its time, fades and vanishes. Its beauty is only of this world.

Seeing ye have purified your souls in your obedience to the truth unto unfeigned love of the brethren, love one another from the heart fervently: having been begotten again, not of corruptible seed, but of incorruptible, through the word of God, which liveth and abideth. For,

> All flesh is as grass,
> and all the glory thereof as the flower of grass.
> The grass withereth, and the flower falleth,
> But the word of the Lord abideth for ever

And this is the word of good tidings which was preached unto you.

The believers should put away any previous childish beliefs, by which is meant the simple beliefs of the Alpha Christians, and accept the Beta teachings which truly lead to salvation. And in these years after the destruction of the Temple, the Christians are also moving into that sacrificial territory. Not only was Christ a sacrifice offered for us, but the believers themselves are a nation of priests, having access to God and doing things that are good in God's sight. They are building a Church which will replace the Temple.

Putting away therefore all wickedness, and all guile, and hypocrisies, and envies, and all evil speakings, as newborn babes, long for the spiritual milk which is without guile, that ye may grow thereby unto salvation; if ye have tasted that the Lord is gracious: unto whom coming, a living stone, rejected indeed of men, but with God elect, precious, ye also, as living stones, are built up a spiritual house, to be a holy priesthood, to offer up spiritual sacrifices, acceptable to God through Jesus Christ. Because it is contained in scripture,

Behold, I lay in Zion a chief corner stone, elect, precious,
and he that believeth on him shall not be put to shame.

For you therefore that believe is the preciousness, but for such as disbelieve, the stone which the builders rejected, the same was made head of the corner, and

a stone of stumbling,
and a rock of offence.

For they stumble at the Word, being disobedient, whereunto also they were appointed. But ye are an elect race, a royal priesthood, a holy nation, a people for [God's] own possession, that ye may show forth the excellencies of him who called you out of darkness into his marvelous light, who in time past were no people, but now are the people of God; who had not obtained mercy, but now have obtained mercy.

Beloved, I beseech you as sojourners and pilgrims, to abstain from fleshly lusts, which war against the soul, having your behavior seemly among the Gentiles; that, wherein they speak against you as evil-doers, they may by your good works, which they behold, glorify God in the day of visitation. Be subject to every ordinance of man for the Lord's sake, whether to the king, as supreme, or unto governors, as sent by him for vengeance on evil-doers and for praise to them that do well. For so is the will of God, that by well-doing ye should put to silence the ignorance of foolish men: as free, and not using your freedom for a cloak of wickedness, but as bondservants of God. Honor all men. Love the brotherhood. Fear God. Honor the king. Servants, [be] in subjection to your masters with all fear; not only to the good and gentle, but also to the froward.

Next, the sermon speaks of the need to suffer adversity patiently, and to respect social conventions, as the best defense against hostility from without.

For this is acceptable, if for conscience toward God a man endureth griefs, suffering wrongfully. For what glory is it, if, when ye sin, and are buffeted [for it], ye shall take it patiently? But if, when ye do well, and suffer [for it], ye shall take it patiently, this is acceptable with God. For hereunto were ye called: because Christ also suffered for you, leaving you an example, that ye should follow his steps: who did no sin, neither was guile found in his mouth: who, when he was reviled, reviled not again; when he suffered threatened not; but committed [himself] to him that judgeth righteously; who his own self bare our sins in his body upon the tree, that we, having died unto sins, might live unto righteousness; by whose stripes ye were healed. For ye were going astray like sheep; but are now returned unto the Shepherd and Bishop of your souls.

In like manner, ye wives, [be] in subjection to your own husbands; that, even if any obey not the word, they may without the word be gained by the behavior of their wives; beholding your chaste behavior [coupled] with fear. Whose [adorning] let it not be the outward adorning of braiding the hair, and of wearing jewels of gold, or of putting on apparel; but [let it be] the hidden man of the heart, in the incorruptible [apparel] of a meek and quiet spirit, which is in the sight of God of great price. For after this manner aforetime the holy women also, who hoped in God, adorned themselves, being in subjection to their own husbands, as Sarah obeyed Abraham, calling him Lord: whose children ye now are, if ye do well, and are not put in fear by any terror. Ye husbands, in like manner, dwell with [your wives] according to knowledge, giving honor unto the woman, as unto the weaker vessel, as being also joint-heirs of the grace of life; to the end that your prayers be not hindered.

Finally, [be] ye all likeminded, compassionate, loving as brethren, tenderhearted, humbleminded: not rendering evil for evil, or reviling for reviling; but contrariwise blessing; for hereunto were ye called, that ye should inherit a blessing. For

He that would love life,
And see good days,
Let him refrain his tongue from evil,
and his lips that they speak no guile.
And let him turn away from evil, and do good;
let him seek peace, and pursue it.

For the eyes of the Lord are upon the righteous,
And his ears unto their supplication:

But the face of the Lord is upon them that do evil.

And who is he that will harm you, if ye be zealous of that which is good?

The sermon ends by returning to the need to suffer patiently, with Christ as a model, and giving a final reminder of the reward to come.

But even if ye should suffer for righteousness' sake, blessed [are ye], and fear not their fear, neither be troubled; but sanctify in your hearts Christ as Lord, [being] ready always to give answer to every man that asketh you a reason concerning the hope that is in you, yet with meekness and fear, having a good conscience; that, wherein ye are spoken against, they may be put to shame who revile your good manner of life in Christ. For it is better, if the will of God should so will, that ye suffer for well-doing than for evil-doing. Because Christ also suffered for sins once, the righteous for the unrighteous, that he might bring us to God; being put to death in the flesh, but made alive in the spirit, in which also he went and preached unto the spirits in prison, that aforetime were disobedient, when the longsuffering of God waited in the days of Noah, while the ark was a preparing, wherein few, that is, eight souls, were saved through water, which also after a true likeness doth now save you, [even] baptism, not the putting away of the filth of the flesh, but the interrogation of a good conscience toward God, through the resurrection of Jesus Christ, who is on the right hand of God, having gone into heaven; angels and authorities and powers being made subject unto him.

Forasmuch then as Christ suffered in the flesh, arm ye yourselves with the same mind; for he that hath suffered in the flesh hath ceased from sin; that ye no longer should live the rest of your time in flesh to the lusts of men, but to the will of God. For the time past may suffice to have wrought the desire of the Gentiles, and to have walked in lasciviousness, lusts, winebibbings, revellings, carousings, and abominable idolatries, wherein they think strange that ye run not with [them] into the same excess of riot, speaking evil of [you], who shall give account to him that is ready to judge the living and the dead. For unto this end was the gospel preached even to the dead, that they might be judged indeed according to men in the flesh, but live according to God in the spirit.

But the end of all things is at hand: be ye therefore of sound mind, and be sober unto prayer: above all things being fervent in your love among yourselves; for love covereth a multitude of sins, using hospitality one to another without murmuring, according as each hath received a gift, ministering it among yourselves, as good stewards of the manifold grace of God, if any man speaketh, [speaking] as it were oracles of God; if any man ministereth, [ministering] as of the strength which God supplieth, that in all things God may be glorified through Jesus Christ, whose is the glory and the dominion for ever and ever. Amen.

———————·••··———————

Reflections

The homily begins, as we might expect, with emphasis on the salvation that has just been assured through becoming a member of the Christian community, and it ends by returning to that same theme: the final glory that is soon to come. In between, it emphasizes the need to imitate Christ in patient obedience, and in enduring suffering. There is emphasis not only on righteousness before God, but on acceptance of human authority and conformity with social expectations, a theme already present in Paul's editors, and in the post-Pauline epistles.

There are some interesting small points. Like the Philippi hymn of old, and like the Gospel of John, soon to come, the Homily thinks of Jesus as existing with God before his life on earth. It also speaks of Jesus preaching to sinners in Hell ("in which [in the spirit] also, he went and preached unto the spirits in prison"), thus taking Jesus out of the limitations of his human existence, and making him a source of life also for those who had died in earlier times. This theme first appears in Colossians, written by Onesimus, and it develops further in the later apocryphal texts. In one version of this "Harrowing of Hell" motif, the only soul left in Hell is that of the hateful Judas. But when Satan boasts that there is one soul which Jesus could not wrest from him, Judas too is saved.[1]

Theologically, the homilist begins with the Resurrection, though he only hints at the more advanced doctrine of the Atonement: like Onesimus in Colossians, he leaves a lot of room for Alpha: for the importance of doing good and avoiding evil.

The final assurance is that the end of all things is at hand, and any want, any hardships, any sufferings, will soon be over. Meanwhile, let each help the other, and the community as a whole will be strengthened for its salvation. Are people saved in groups? No, but a group can be either more or less supportive of its members, and in that way can be very important to an individual's salvation. Our homilist is making that point here. A church leader knows what function a church or a community has, in that larger scheme of things.

The sermon conveys confidence in its theology, and in its expectation of salvation. From that position, it offers practical instruction to the new members. But the times were perilous. In a few years, the homilist will return to his homily, and send it out again with counsel about a new and dire emergency.

All that lies in the future. For now, though relations with the parent religion could not be called cordial, there was still something of a modus vivendi between the two factions within the Jesus sect..

[1] In the Acts of Andrew and Paul; see the summary in Elliott **Apocryphal** 302.

48. Toleration in the Synagogues
Tosephta Shabbat 13:5

Up to this point, Christians had continued to be Jews, and as such to take part in synagogue worship. Their texts, if any (one was probably the Gospel of Mark, their first authority statement; another may have been a copy of the circular letter of Jacob), were accordingly sometimes kept in the synagogue. Grand synagogue buildings, meant to replace the Temple whose rebuilding was no longer a viable possibility, were rare until the 3rd century. Before then, especially in the smaller towns, Jews may have met in someone's house, just as the Jesus followers did. One way or another, the first century situation was that members of the Jesus sect often kept their special texts in the same place as the more mainstream Jews did. This we know because the Rabbinic texts provide for it, by specifying what should be rescued from a fire. The Rabbis disapproved of the Jesus texts, and had hard words for them, but the hard words attest the presence of the texts. The fact that these Jesus texts contained the name of God, which had to be treated with respect, was a complication. Here are several rulings on the issue, by two named Rabbis:

The books of the Evangelists and the books of the minim they do not save from a fire. But they are allowed to burn where they are. They and the references to the Divine Name in them.

Rabbi Yose the Galilean says, On ordinary days, one cuts out the references to the Divine Name which are in them and stores them away, and the rest burns.

Said Rabbi Tarfon, May I bury my sons, if such things come into my hands and I do not burn them, and even the references to the Divine Name which are in them.

———————••••———————

Reflections

The God in the Jesus texts, starting with the Gospel of Mark, was the same God worshiped by all Jews. The Jesus sect was thus an internal problem, the hardest kind of problem to deal with.

For a while, the tension created by this disturbing textual presence went uncorrected. Under Yoḥanan, the Jesus people were still tolerated. Since the problem was there to be decided, it must be that Jesus sect writings were at least sometimes kept in the synagogues, alongside the recognized Scriptures.

That practical toleration would eventually change under Gamaliel II, Yoḥanan's successor at Yabneh.

Meanwhile, the Jesus sect leaders were working with their own mixed doctrinal heritage: Alpha along with Beta, faith contending with works as the key to salvation. This slumbering opposition, papered over by Paul's editors,[1] would presently break out. Meanwhile, Paul's onetime manager Onesimus, a man of peace and an adroit manager, presides over another delicate balance by keeping the Alpha/Beta compromise steady for the Christians of Ephesus, whose Bishop he has just become.

[1]See Chapter 41.

49. A Hymn to the Light
Ephesians 5:8-14

Onesimus, Paul's manager in Ephesus and the chief editor of his letters, wrote Colossians[1] as a sort of preface to that collection. It was in a distinctively heavy style of Greek. Later, most likely on the occasion of his becoming Bishop of Ephesus, he wrote Ephesians, a letter of "Paul" to that city. It is in the same heavy style of Greek, and amounts to an update and extension of Colossians.

Colossians had contained a hymn, and Ephesians also contains a hymn, or at least an echo of a fragment of a hymn: a hymn to the Light, to which those who are saved will one day awake. The preceding verses emphasize right doing as the way to salvation, and are thus consistent with the Alpha point of view. The hymn occupies only one verse in Ephesians. Here it is in context:

. . . For ye were once darkness, but now light in the Lord; walk as children of light, for the fruit of the light is in all goodness and righteousness and truth, proving what is well-pleasing unto the Lord. And have no fellowship with the unfruitful works of darkness, but rather even reprove them, for the things which are done by them in secret it is a shame even to speak of. But all things when they are reproved are made manifest by the light, for everything that is made manifest is light. Wherefore he saith,

> Awake, thou that sleepeth,
> And arise from the dead,
> and Christ shall shine upon thee.

---

[1]Colossae was the city where Onesimus himself had been a slave; in Colossians, he writes out of knowledge of the local situation, as it had been in Paul's lifetime. (Colossae no longer existed when Onesimus wrote that letter, it had been destroyed, with Laodicea and Hierapolis, by an earthquake shortly after Paul's death in 60).

Reflections

This piece, with its Light images, may remind us of "nor is anything secret, except to come to light" in Jesus' Sermon by the Sea. But it looks ahead more strongly to the Light and Life linkage which we meet in the Gospel of John:

In him was Life, and the Life was the Light of men, and the Light shineth in the darkness, and the darkness apprehended it not . . . there was the true Light, which lighteth every man, coming into the world. (John 1:4, 9)

Which side of the Alpha/Beta war does Onesimus take, in this letter? Does he say, with Paul, that works are nothing, and acceptance of the atoning death of Jesus is everything? To judge from the opening of Ephesians, Yes, he does:

Blessed be the God and Father of our Lord Jesus Christ, who hath blessed us with every spiritual blessing in the heavenly places in Christ, even as he chose us in him before the foundation of the world, that we should be holy and without blemish before him in love; having foreordained us unto adoption as sons through Jesus Christ unto himself, according to the good pleasure of his will, to the praise of the glory of his grace, which he freely bestowed on us in the Beloved, in whom we have our redemption through his blood, the forgiveness of our trespasses, according to the riches of his grace . . . (Ephesians 1:3-7)

The Beta signs in this are the blood of Christ, and grace, plus predestination.

But there, Onesimus is speaking in the persona of Paul. Later on, the text takes a different turn: it criticizes evil deeds, and recommends that its hearers do them no more, and turn to good works. This puts us back in Alpha territory. Ephesians ends with a final Pauline touch: the taking up of weapons:

And put on the whole armor of God, that ye may be able to stand against the wiles of the Devil. (Ephesians 6:11)

Even here, there is nothing about faith, but much of resolution in right doing.

No theory of salvation can entirely do without a preference for good deeds over evil ones. We here see Onesimus in his own work, as he had sought to do in his editorial work, blending the rival ideas of Alpha and Beta.

The classic integration of the "light" motif with developing Jesus tradition is to be found only a few years later, in the Gospel of John.

50. Light and Life
John 1:1-6

The Gospel of John is the end product of the line of rival Gospels. It is sometimes said of it, "John finally got it right." Not in John do we struggle with internal contradictions; everything is consistent. There is no more Davidic Messiah stuff; the Cleansing of the Temple, which in Mark was the focus of Jesus' move on Jerusalem, is here transferred to an earlier year, and has nothing like that meaning. Nor does the Johannine Jesus, halfway through the story (as in Mark and the rest), suddenly decide that he is going to die. Jesus in John, from beginning to end, has in view his "glorification," as this Gospel calls it; his being "lifted up" in the new sense of returning to the Father. And in that emphasis on the return, we can see that John is the heir of the line of thought which we have glimpsed in the Philippi hymn, some forty years earlier. Jesus is not of this world; he is a sojourner. His real existence is heavenly.

The Gospel of John is heavenly too. It is lit by light from another star. Everything is seen with intense clarity, but it is an unreal clarity. It follows the ideas of Philo of Alexandria, who identified Jewish tradition with the cosmos, the Logos, the Word. Not the Word of Mark's Gospel (the teaching of Jesus), but the Word spoken at the Creation, which itself created all things.

John's Gospel opens with a lyrical statement of that identity:

In the beginning was the Word, and the Word was with God, and the Word was God. The same was in the beginning with God. All things were made through him; and without him was not anything made that hath been made. In him was life; and the life was the light of men. And the light shineth in the darkness; and the darkness apprehended it not.

———————••••••———————

Reflections

As this hymnlike meditation goes on, it gradually dissolves into the coming of John the Baptist as Jesus' precursor, an almost cinematic technique.

In this last of the Gospels, there is no suggestion that Jesus might have been John's disciple. On the contrary, the baptism of Jesus is not even recounted, and as soon as Jesus appears in person, John's disciples begin to defect to him. Jesus is no longer in competition with John; *Jesus is the whole story.*

The cosmic eternity of this opening permeates the rest of the text. All is consistent, especially Jesus' idea of himself, which he preaches relentlessly; there is no variation or turning. Some people are interested in Jesus' message and some are not, but the story moves to its end regardless. And Jesus at the Crucifixion does not end in despair, as in Mark. He goes through the motions: the parting of the garments, the offering of the vinegar; the fulfilment of Scripture. And then, his last word: "It is finished." Jesus bowed his head in submission to the higher plan for him, and "gave up his spirit."

The absence of pain from the Crucifixion scene has been noticed, and a special term has been made for it: "docetism," the idea that Jesus on earth only *seemed* (Greek δοκεω) human. That term, like so many theological coinages, has implications and controversies, into which we need not enter here.

There is a touching moment in the Crucifixion scene, one unique to John, when Jesus, seeing Mary among the spectators, commends her thereafter to the care of a disciple, with the words "Behold, thy mother!" And from that moment the disciple takes her into his home.

This is not all John does, to bring the family of Jesus back into the picture. Since he regards Jesus as existing from the beginning of time, there is no place in his Gospel for a Birth of Jesus scene. But he finds other ways.

51. The Wedding at Cana
John 2:1-11

There has been little of domestic interest in the foregoing chapters; on the contrary, the early Gospels constantly emphasize the need to separate from family and friends. All the more welcome is this first "sign" of Jesus' career; the first time – at least, as John tells it – when he displays his power.

The mother of Jesus, who has figured in no previous account of his career, is there with him, and this is how it went:

And the third day there was a marriage in Cana of Galilee; and the mother of Jesus was there: and Jesus also was bidden, and his disciples, to the marriage. And when the wine failed, the mother of Jesus saith unto him, They have no wine. And Jesus saith unto her, Woman, what have I to do with thee? Mine hour is not yet come. His mother saith unto the servants, Whatsoever he saith unto you, do it. Now there were six waterpots of stone set there after the Jews' manner of purifying, containing two or three firkins apiece. Jesus saith unto them, Fill the waterpots with water. And they filled them up to the brim. And he saith unto them, Draw out now, and bear unto the ruler of the feast. And they bare it. And when the ruler of the feast tasted the water now become wine, and knew not whence it was (but the servants that had drawn the water knew), the ruler of the feast calleth the bridegroom, and saith unto him, Every man setteth on first the good wine; and when [men] have drunk freely, [then] that which is worse; thou hast kept the good wine until now.

This beginning of his signs did Jesus in Cana of Galilee, and manifested his glory; and his disciples believed on him.

Reflections

John is intimately aware of Mark, but though he sometimes repeats Mark, more often, as here, he goes further and transforms Mark.

Jesus in Mark had rejected his mother and his brothers, and identified instead with his new family: those who "hear the word of God and do it." This is pretty brusque. Can't Jesus be a little less brusque? After all, it's his mother.

The Gospels steadily give more space to feelings in favor of Jesus' mother. Mark, if anything, is negative. She gets a key role in Matthew's Birth Narrative, and top billing in Luke's remake of that story. But even in Luke, the only appearance of Mary *in the story* is to be rejected by Jesus, in the passage still retained from Mark. In John, all this is transformed. There is no rejection of Jesus' mother. She is present at his Crucifixion.

And she is present at this Cana story. If we look at that story more closely, we see a trace of the Markan Jesus. Mary clearly expects him to do a miracle; Jesus sulks. He complains, My time is not yet come. A typical pushy mother, she goes ahead anyway, telling the wine stewards to do what he tells them. Jesus, socially trapped, obliges with the miracle of making wine out of water. This is an insulated miracle; it produces no result in the wine steward, or the wedding guests, or anybody else. His disciples, who as far as we know already believe in him, or else they wouldn't be there, seemingly believe a little more. The episode has a perfunctory quality. The only detail with any substance to it is the relation between sulky Jesus and his proud mother.

The sulky Jesus in this story has been thought to be a forerunner of the Brat Jesus in the Infancy Gospel of Thomas, who responds to being bumped by killing the child who bumped him, or to being scolded by killing the teacher who scolded him.[1] That is less ridiculous than it may seem. What woman among the Infancy Gospel readership would not be inwardly pleased to see how child Jesus takes nothing from nobody, not his playmates, or even his teacher? What woman reader would not like the way Mary takes charge at Cana?

There do not seem to be any female *writers*, in these early Christian texts, but the importance of their female *audience* can hardly be overestimated.

All told, this Cana story looks like a transformed and female-friendly echo of Jesus' rejection of his mother in Mark. Nor was the reprocessing of other people's texts confined to the Gospels. It was more or less the order of the day.

---

[1]For these episodes, see Elliott **Apocryphal** 76-77.

52. An Alpha Statement
1 John, original

In the late Eighties,[1] an unknown Alpha pastor wrote this letter to remind his Alpha hearers of their basic beliefs, and give some further counsel.

[CLAIMING APOSTOLIC AUTHORITY]

That which was from the beginning, that which we have heard, that which we have seen with our eyes, that which we beheld and our hands handled,[2] concerning the Word of Life, (and the Life was manifested, and we have seen, and bear witness, and declare unto you the Life, the eternal Life which was with the Father, and was manifested unto us). And these things we write, that our joy may be made full.

[SIN AND FORGIVENESS]

And this is the message we have heard from him and announce unto you, that God is light, and in him is no darkness at all. If we say that we have fellowship with him and walk in the darkness, we lie, and do not the truth. If we say that we have no sin, we deceive ourselves, and the truth is not in us. If we confess our sins, he is faithful and righteous to forgive us our sins, and to cleanse us from all unrighteousness. If we say we have not sinned, we make Him a liar, and His Word is not in us. My little children, these things write I unto you that ye may not sin. And hereby we know that we know him: if we keep his commandments. He that saith, I know him, and keepeth not his commandments, is a liar, and the truth is not in him. But whoso keepeth his Word, in him verily hath the love of God been perfected.

[THE COMMANDMENT OF BROTHERLY LOVE]

Beloved, no new commandment write I unto you, but an old commandment, which ye had from the beginning: the old commandment is the Word which ye heard. He that saith he is in the light and hateth his brother, is in the darkness even until now. He that loveth his brother abideth in the light, and there is no occasion of stumbling in him. But he that hateth his brother is in the darkness, and walketh in the darkness, and knoweth not whither he goeth, because the darkness hath blinded his eyes.

---

[1]This letter is not by the author of the Gospel of John; that is an inference from the fact that it is closely related to the Gospel. Some ideas in the letter (in its Beta-adapted form, for which see Chapter 53) were inserted into a late layer of the Gospel of John. That relation dates the Beta form to c90; this original Alpha form is slightly earlier.

[2]This amounts to a claim that the author is one of the original companions of Jesus. Toward the end of the century, such Apostolic claims were increasingly necessary to get a hearing for a text. The end of the Apostolic Age spawned an Apostolic Literature.

[WARNING AGAINST WORLDLY TEMPTATIONS]

I have written unto you, little children, because ye know the Father. I have written unto you, fathers, because ye know him who is from the beginning. I have written unto you, young men, because ye are strong, and the Word of God abideth in you, and ye have overcome the Evil One. Love not the world, neither the things that are in the world. If any man love the world, the love of the Father is not in him. For all that is in the world, the lust of the flesh and the lust of the eyes and the vain glory of life, is not of the Father, but is of the world. And the world passeth away, and the lust thereof, but he that doeth the will of God abideth forever.

[WARNING AGAINST FALSE TEACHERS]

And ye have an anointing from the Holy One, and ye know all the things. I have not written unto you because ye know not the truth, but because ye know it, and because no lie is of the truth. As for you, let that abide in you which ye heard from the beginning. And this is the promise which he promised us: the life eternal. These things have I written unto you concerning them that would lead you astray.

[THE ANOINTING FROM GOD]

And as for you, the anointing which ye received of him abideth in you, and ye need not that any one teach you, but as his anointing teacheth you, concerning all things, and is true, and is no lie, and even as it taught you, ye abide in him. And now, little children, abide in him, that if he shall be manifested, we may have boldness, and not be ashamed before him at his coming. If ye know that he is righteous, ye know that every one also that doeth righteousness is begotten of him.

[THE CHILDREN OF GOD]

Behold what manner of love the Father hath bestowed upon us, that we should be called children of God, and [such] we are. For this cause the world knoweth us not, because it knew him not. Beloved, now are we children of God, and it is not yet made manifest what we shall be. We know that, if he shall be manifested, we shall be like him, for we shall see him, even as he is. And every one that hath this hope [set] on him purifieth himself, even as he is pure. Every one that doeth sin doeth also lawlessness, and sin is lawlessness. Whosoever abideth in him sinneth not; whosoever sinneth hath not seen him, neither knoweth him. Little children, let no man lead you astray: he that doeth righteousness is righteous, even as he is righteous; he that doeth sin is of the devil, for the devil sinneth from the beginning. Whosover is begotten of God doeth no sin, because his seed abideth in him, and he cannot sin, because he is begotten of God. In this the children of God are manifest, and the children of the devil: whosoever doeth not righteousness is not of God, neither he that loveth not his brother.

[HATRED OF BROTHERS]

For this is the message which ye heard from the beginning: that we should love one another, not as Cain was of the evil one, and slew his brother. And wherefore slew he him? Because his works were evil, and his brother's righteous. Marvel not, brethren, if the world hateth you. We know that we have passed out of death into life, because we love the brethren. He that loveth not abideth in death. Whosoever hateth his brother is a murderer, and ye know that no murderer hath eternal life abiding in him. But whoso hath the world's goods, and beholdeth his brother in need, and shutteth up his compassion from him, how doth the love of God abide in him? Little children, let us not love in word, neither with the tongue; but in deed and truth. Hereby shall we know that we are of the truth, and shall assure our heart before him, because if our heart condemn us, God is greater than our heart, and knoweth all things. Beloved, if our heart condemn us not, we have boldness toward God; and whatsoever we ask we receive of him, because we keep his commandments and do the things that are pleasing in his sight. And he that keepeth his commandments abideth in him, and he in him. And hereby we know that he abideth in us, by the Spirit which he gave us.

[PROVING THE SPIRITS]

Beloved, believe not every spirit, but prove the spirits, whether they are of God, because many false prophets are gone out into the world. Ye are of God, little children, and have overcome them, because greater is he that is in you than he that is in the world. They are of the world, therefore speak they of the world, and the world heareth them. We are of God: he that knoweth God heareth us; he who is not of God heareth us not. By this we know the spirit of truth, and the spirit of error.

[ENCOURAGEMENT TO LOVE THE BROTHERS]

Beloved, let us love one another, for love is of God, and every one that loveth is begotten of God, and knoweth God. He that loveth not knoweth not God, for God is love. No man hath beheld God at any time; if we love one another, God abideth in us, and his love is perfected in us. And we know and have believed the love which God hath in us. God is love, and he that abideth in love abideth in God, and God abideth in him. Herein is love made perfect with us, that we may have boldness in the day of judgment; because as he is, even so are we in this world. There is no fear in love, but perfect love casteth out fear, because fear hath punishment, and he that feareth is not made perfect in love. We love, because he first loved us. If a man say, I love God, and hateth his brother, he is a liar, for he that loveth not his brother whom he hath seen, cannot love God whom he hath not seen. And this commandment have we from him, that he who loveth God love his brother also. Hereby we know that we love the children of God, when we love God and do his commandments. For this is the love of God, that we keep his commandments, and his commandments are not grievous. For whosoever is begotten of God overcometh the world, and this is the victory that hath overcome the world, [even] our faith.

[ASSURANCE OF THE GRANTING OF PRAYER]

And this is the boldness which we have toward him: that, if we ask anything according to his will, he heareth us; and if we know that he heareth us whatsoever we ask, we know that we have the petitions which we have asked of him.

[PRAYING FOR THE ERRING BROTHER]

If any man see his brother sinning a sin not unto death, he shall ask, and [God] will give him life for them that sin not unto death. There is a sin unto death; not concerning this do I say that he should make request. All unrighteousness is sin, and there is a sin not unto death. We know that whosoever is begotten of God sinneth not; but he that was begotten of God keepeth himself, and the evil one toucheth him not. We know that we are of God, and the whole world lieth in the evil one.

[WARNING AGAINST IDOLATRY]

[My] little children, guard yourselves from idols.

———————··•··———————

Reflections

Much of this is familiar Alpha territory. We can see that the writer follows closely the model of the Epistle of Jacob, down to the almost final comment on the erring brother. (Though, as time passes and doctrine hardens, we discover that there are sins of the erring brother from which he cannot be redeemed).

Notable in this letter are the opening claim of Apostolic authorship, the confidence ("boldness") of the saved in their Sonship, which permits them to ask anything of the Father, and the ideal of loving the brethren. This last has by now become standard with the Beta Christians also. Its survival value for any embattled group is obvious, and neither side seems to have neglected it.

Another thread that runs through the letter is the danger of those who would teach otherwise. The warning was timely. Those who would teach otherwise would soon lay hands on this Alpha statement, and convert it into a Beta one.

53. A Beta Appropriation
1 John, expanded with Beta interpolations

Those who would teach otherwise were watching. A spokesman for the other side inserted into that letter a series of corrections which converted it into a Beta statement. These additions can be easily detected because many of them simply reverse the original. To see how this works, here is the original letter again, but now with the insertions in place, as we find them in our Bibles. Insertions are indented, and key Beta terms are italicized for easy recognition.

[CLAIMING APOSTOLIC AUTHORITY]

That which was from the beginning, that which we have heard, that which we have seen with our eyes, that which we beheld and our hands handled, concerning the Word of Life, (and the Life was manifested, and we have seen, and bear witness, and declare unto you the Life, the eternal Life which was with the Father, and was manifested unto us).

> that which we have seen and heard declare we unto you also, that ye also may have fellowship with us; yea, and our fellowship is with the Father, *and with his Son Jesus Christ.*[1]

And these things we write, that our joy may be made full.

[SIN AND FORGIVENESS]

And this is the message we have heard from him and announce unto you, that God is light, and in him is no darkness at all. If we say that we have fellowship with him and walk in the darkness, we lie, and do not the truth.

> But if we walk in the light, as he is in the light, we have fellowship one with another, *and the blood of Jesus his Son cleanseth us from all sin.*[2]

If we say that we have no sin, we deceive ourselves, and the truth is not in us. If we confess our sins, he is faithful and righteous to forgive us our sins, and to cleanse us from all unrighteousness. If we say we have not sinned, we make Him a liar, and His Word is not in us. My little children, these things write I unto you that ye may not sin.

> And if any man sin, we have *an advocate*[3] *with the Father, Jesus Christ the righteous; and he is the propitiation for our sins, and not for ours only, but also for the whole world.*[4]

---

[1] Intruding Jesus into what was originally the relation between believers and God.

[2] The root Atonement doctrine: it is the blood of Christ, not God, that forgives sins.

[3] This is the usual sense of "Paraclete." It is found also in John 15. For John 16, a later chapter, where a different sense occurs, see Chapter 58, page 161.

[4] Jesus is the universal Saviour; there is no relationship with the individual.

And hereby we know that we know him: if we keep his commandments. He that saith, I know him, and keepeth not his commandments, is a liar, and the truth is not in him. But whoso keepeth his Word, in him verily hath the love of God been perfected.

Hereby we know that we are in him: he that saith he abideth in him ought himself also to walk *even as he walked.*[5]

[THE COMMANDMENT OF BROTHERLY LOVE]

Beloved, no new commandment write I unto you, but an old commandment, which ye had from the beginning: the old commandment is the Word which ye heard.

Again, a new commandment write I unto you, which thing is true in him and in you, because the darkness is passing away, and *the true light already shineth.*

He that saith he is in the light and hateth his brother, is in the darkness even until now. He that loveth his brother abideth in the light, and there is no occasion of stumbling in him. But he that hateth his brother is in the darkness, and walketh in the darkness, and knoweth not whither he goeth, because the darkness hath blinded his eyes.

I write unto you, little children, because your sins are forgiven you *for his name's sake.* I write unto you, fathers, because ye know him who is from the beginning. I write unto you, young men, because ye have overcome the Evil One.[6]

[WARNING AGAINST WORLDLY TEMPTATIONS]

I have written unto you, little children, because ye know the Father. I have written unto you, fathers, because ye know him who is from the beginning. I have written unto you, young men, because ye are strong, and the Word of God abideth in you, and ye have overcome the Evil One. Love not the world, neither the things that are in the world. If any man love the world, the love of the Father is not in him. For all that is in the world, the lust of the flesh and the lust of the eyes and the vain glory of life, is not of the Father, but is of the world. And the world passeth away, and the lust thereof, but he that doeth the will of God abideth forever.

Little children, it is the last hour, and as ye heard that *Antichrist* cometh, even now have there arisen many Antichrists, whereby we know it is the last hour. They *went out from us,*[7] but they were not of us, for if they had been of us, they would have continued with us, but they went out, that they might be made manifest that they all are not of us.

---

[5] Imitation of Jesus, rather than obedience to God. Again, as commonly in Beta, Jesus intrudes into what used to be a relation between man and God.

[6] This is the only place in the text where a Beta section anticipates an Alpha section.

[7] For what is probably this Alpha/Beta schism, see the next chapter.

[WARNING AGAINST FALSE TEACHERS]

And ye have an anointing from the Holy One, and ye know all the things. I have not written unto you because ye know not the truth, but because ye know it, and because no lie is of the truth.

Who is the liar but he that denieth that *Jesus is the Christ*? This is the *Antichrist*, [even] he that denieth the Father and the Son. Whosoever *denieth the Son*, the same hath not the Father; *he that confesseth the Son hath the Father also.*

As for you, let that abide in you which ye heard from the beginning.

If that which ye heard from the beginning abide in you, ye also shall *abide in the Son*, and in the Father.

And this is the promise which he promised us: the life eternal. These things have I written unto you concerning them that would lead you astray.

[THE ANOINTING FROM GOD]

And as for you, the anointing which ye received of him abideth in you, and ye need not that any one teach you, but as his anointing teacheth you, concerning all things, and is true, and is no lie, and even as it taught you, ye abide in him. And now, little children, abide in him, that if he shall be manifested, we may have boldness, and not be ashamed before him at his coming. If ye know that he is righteous, ye know that every one also that doeth righteousness is begotten of him.

[THE CHILDREN OF GOD]

Behold what manner of love the Father hath bestowed upon us, that we should be called children of God, and [such] we are. For this cause the world knoweth us not, because it knew him not. Beloved, now are we children of God, and it is not yet made manifest what we shall be. We know that, if he shall be manifested, we shall be like him, for we shall see him, even as he is. And every one that hath this hope [set] on him purifieth himself, even as he is pure. Every one that doeth sin doeth also lawlessness, and sin is lawlessness.

And ye know that *he was manifested to take away* sins; and in him is no sin.

Whosoever abideth in him sinneth not; whosoever sinneth hath not seen him, neither knoweth him. Little children, let no man lead you astray: he that doeth righteousness is righteous, even as he is righteous; he that doeth sin is of the devil, for the devil sinneth from the beginning.

To this end *was the Son of God manifested*, that he might destroy the works of the devil.[8]

Whosover is begotten of God doeth no sin, because his seed abideth in him, and he cannot sin, because he is begotten of God. In this the children of God are manifest, and the children of the devil: whosoever doeth not righteousness is not of God, neither he that loveth not his brother.

---

[8]This cosmic conflict model is characteristic of Beta thinking.

[HATRED OF BROTHERS]

For this is the message which ye heard from the beginning: that we should love one another, not as Cain was of the evil one, and slew his brother. And wherefore slew he him? Because his works were evil, and his brother's righteous. Marvel not, brethren, if the world hateth you. We know that we have passed out of death into life, because we love the brethren. He that loveth not abideth in death. Whosoever hateth his brother is a murderer, and ye know that no murderer hath eternal life abiding in him.

> Hereby know we love, because *he laid down his* life *for us*, and we ought to lay down our lives for the brethren.[9]

But whoso hath the world's goods, and beholdeth his brother in need, and shutteth up his compassion from him, how doth the love of God abide in him? Little children, let us not love in word, neither with the tongue; but in deed and truth. Hereby shall we know that we are of the truth, and shall assure our heart before him, because if our heart condemn us, God is greater than our heart, and knoweth all things. Beloved, if our heart condemn us not, we have boldness toward God; and whatsoever we ask we receive of him, because we keep his commandments and do the things that are pleasing in his sight.

> And this is his commandment, that we should *believe in the name of his Son Jesus Christ*, and love one another, even as he gave us commandment.[10]

And he that keepeth his commandments abideth in him, and he in him. And hereby we know that he abideth in us, by the Spirit which he gave us.

[PROVING THE SPIRITS]

Beloved, believe not every spirit, but prove the spirits, whether they are of God,[11] because many false prophets are gone out into the world.

> Hereby know ye the Spirit of God: every spirit that *confesseth that Jesus Christ is come in the flesh* is of God, and every spirit that *confesseth not Jesus is not of God*, and this is the [spirit] of the *Antichrist*, whereof ye have heard that it cometh, and now it is in the world already.[12]

Ye are of God, little children, and have overcome them, because greater is he that is in you than he that is in the world. They are of the world, therefore speak they of the world, and the world heareth them. We are of God: he that knoweth God heareth us; he who is not of God heareth us not. By this we know the spirit of truth, and the spirit of error.

---

[9]Every good deed of the Beta believer is good because it imitates Christ.

[10]The prime commandment, for the Beta believer, is to believe in the Atonement.

[11]As the Didache had counseled. See Chapter 16, page 47.

[12]The Didache knows nothing of this concept, but those who do not accept it are here identified with Satan. The temperature between these opponents is being raised.

[ENCOURAGEMENT TO LOVE THE BROTHERS]

Beloved, let us love one another, for love is of God, and every one that loveth is begotten of God, and knoweth God. He that loveth not knoweth not God, for God is love.

Herein was the love of God manifested in us: *that God hath sent his only begotten Son into the world that we might live through him.* Herein is love, not that we loved God, but that he loved us, and *sent his Son [to be] the propitiation for our sins.* Beloved, if God so loved us, we also ought to love one another.

No man hath beheld God at any time; if we love one another, God abideth in us, and his love is perfected in us.

Hereby we know that we abide in him and he in us, because he hath given us of his Spirit. And we have beheld and bear witness that the Father hath sent the Son [to be] the Saviour of the world. Whosoever shall *confess that Jesus is the Son of God,* God abideth in him, and he in God.

And we know and have believed the love which God hath in us. God is love, and he that abideth in love abideth in God, and God abideth in him. Herein is love made perfect with us, that we may have boldness in the day of judgment; because as he is, even so are we in this world. There is no fear in love, but perfect love casteth out fear, because fear hath punishment, and he that feareth is not made perfect in love. We love, because he first loved us. If a man say, I love God, and hateth his brother, he is a liar, for he that loveth not his brother whom he hath seen, cannot love God whom he hath not seen. And this commandment have we from him, that he who loveth God love his brother also.

Whosoever *believeth that Jesus is the Christ is begotten of God,* and whosoever loveth him that begat loveth him also that is begotten of him.

Hereby we know that we love the children of God, when we love God and do his commandments. For this is the love of God, that we keep his commandments, and his commandments are not grievous. For whosoever is begotten of God overcometh the world, and this is the victory that hath overcome the world, [even] our faith.

And who is he that overcometh the world, but he that *believeth that Jesus is the Son of God?* This is he that came *by water and blood,* [even] *Jesus Christ*; not with the water only, but with the *water and with the blood.* If we receive the witness of men, the witness of God is greater, for the witness of God is this, that he *hath borne witness concerning his Son.* He that *believeth on the Son of God hath the witness in him*; he that believeth not, God hath made him a liar, because he hath not believed in *the witness that God hath borne concerning his Son.* And the witness is this, that God gave unto us eternal life, and *this life is in his Son.* He that *hath the Son* hath the life; he that hath not the Son of God hath not the life. These things have I written unto you, that ye may know that ye have eternal life, [even] unto you that *believe on the name of the Son of God.*

[ASSURANCE OF THE GRANTING OF PRAYER]

And this is the boldness which we have toward him: that, if we ask anything according to his will, he heareth us; and if we know that he heareth us whatsoever we ask, we know that we have the petitions which we have asked of him.

[PRAYING FOR THE ERRING BROTHER]

If any man see his brother sinning a sin not unto death, he shall ask, and [God] will give him life for them that sin not unto death. There is a sin unto death; not concerning this do I say that he should make request. All unrighteousness is sin, and there is a sin not unto death. We know that whosoever is begotten of God sinneth not; but he that was begotten of God keepeth himself, and the evil one toucheth him not. We know that we are of God, and the whole world lieth in the evil one.

And we know that the Son of God is come, and hath given us an understanding, that we know him that is true, and we are in him that is true, [even] in *his Son Jesus Christ*. This is the true God, and eternal life.

[WARNING AGAINST IDOLATRY]

[My] little children, guard yourselves from idols.

Reflections

Here is how one faction can infiltrate the camp of another faction, and change that faction's codes. This particular instance represents a new faction (the Beta or Resurrection and Atonement faction) co-opting an older faction. Matthew had sought to appropriate the Hebrew Scriptures to Christian uses. Some Beta spokesman is here doing much the same with an Alpha document. It is much easier to make use of existing documents, than to make up your own.

It is common in religious movements that an original belief in time becomes a heresy.[13] In this case, the early Alpha belief is not excluded; it is *subverted,* so as to make it preach the Beta orthodoxy.

And there were other signs of the breakout of the old Alpha/Beta argument. Not only in doctrinal statements such as 1 John, but in the equally sensitive area of church administration.

It has come to this: Who owns the churches?

---

[13]For the general phenomenon in Christianity, see Bauer **Orthodoxy**. Hatred among brethren (those within) can often be more intense than any hatred of mere outsiders. There is a sense not only of opposition, but of betrayal.

54. A Beta Refusal
2 John

With the previous demonstration of strife within Christianity before us, it is easy to see that these two letters reflect opposing sides of the Alpha/Beta split. We may take them in canonical order.

The elder unto the elect lady and her children, whom I love in truth; and not I only, but also all they that know the truth; for the truth's sake which abideth in us, and it shall be with us for ever: Grace, mercy, peace shall be with us, from God the Father, and from Jesus Christ, the Son of the Father, in truth and love.

I rejoice greatly that I have found [certain] of thy children walking in truth, even as we received commandment from the Father. And now I beseech thee, lady, not as though I wrote to thee a new commandment, but that which we had from the beginning,[1] that we love one another. And this is love, that we should walk after his commandments. This is the commandment, even as ye heard from the beginning, that ye should walk in it. For many deceivers are gone forth into the world, [even] they that confess not that Jesus Christ cometh in the flesh. This is the deceiver and the Antichrist.[2] Look to yourselves, that ye lose not the things which we have wrought, but that ye receive a full reward. Whosoever goeth onward and abideth not in the teaching of Christ, hath not God: he that abideth in the teaching, the same hath both the Father and the Son.

If any one cometh unto you, and bringeth not this teaching, receive him not into [your] house, and give him no greeting: for he that giveth him greeting partaketh in his evil works.[3]

Having many things to write unto you, I would not [write them] with paper and ink: but I hope to come unto you, and to speak face to face, that your joy may be made full. The children of thine elect sister salute thee.

———————•••••———————

[1] Readers of Chapter 52 (page 141) will recognize this phrase.

[2] The Antichrist is a distinctive Beta concept; see pages 146-147.

[3] No more fellowship, no contact, with the hated ones who believe differently. This is where the old Alpha/Beta conflict, briefly papered over by Paul's editors (page 115), comes loose again, and causes an open rupture.

Reflections

This and the next letter, 3 John, are evidently a compositional pair, and must have been written at the same time. A phrase at the end of 3 John, "thou knowesrt that our witness is true," echoes a phrase at the end of the Gospel of John, "This is the disciple that beareth witness of these things, and we know that his witness is true" (Jn 21:24). That chapter, John 21, overrides Jn 20:31, the natural ending of the Gospel ("but these are written, that ye may believe that Jesus is the Christ, the Son of God, and that, believing, ye may have life in his name"), and is therefore a final appendage to the Gospel. Then we have the following chronological relationship:

John [early layers] > 1 John > John [later layers] > John 21 > 2 and 3 John

This is the best we can do on the internal evidence. The author, or authors, of 2 and 3 John, the author of the original Alpha version of 1 John, the Beta reviser of 1 John, and the author of the Gospel, seem to be different persons. There are literary relations among these texts, and they are rightly grouped together in our Bibles, but there is no literal unity of authorship.

The "elect lady" is another church to which the unnamed "elder" (whom we are to take as a leading figure in his own church) is writing. The "elect" part implies predestination, which is not technically compatible with Alpha belief, according to which you have to earn your salvation, and you may perhaps fail. Thus our suspicion that this letter is composed from a Beta point of view.

The hatred for those who think wrongly, in this letter, and its repeated insistence that what these two churches have in common is the "truth," are typical of the hardening of doctrine in these years, beginning soon after the end of the Apostolic Age. Those who think wrongly are no longer erring brothers to be wooed back into the community, as the Epistle of Jacob recommended:[4] they are the Antichrist, the Devil incarnate, and any contact with them defiles.

As mentioned in the notes, the signature statement of the Betas is still the assertion that God can be reached *only through Jesus*. Jesus has expanded to fill the cosmos, and to block every other possible access to God. This kind of outrageous theological exaggeration, eliminating all other access to God, may have strained the delicate relation between the Jesus sect and its Jewish parent to the breaking point.

[4]See Chapter 15 (page 43).

55. An Alpha Response
3 John

Here is the twin of the previous letter. Its author and his recipient appear to be on the receiving end of whatever is going on.

The elder[1] unto Gaius the beloved, whom I love in truth. Beloved, I pray that in all things thou mayest prosper and be in health, even as thy soul prospereth. For I rejoiced greatly, when brethren came and bare witness unto thy truth, even as thou walkest in truth.[2] Greater joy have I none than this, to hear of my children walking in the truth. Beloved, thou doest a faithful work in whatsoever thou doest toward them that are brethren and strangers withal; who bare witness to thy love before the church: whom thou wilt do well to set forward on their journey worthily of God: because that for the sake of the Name they went forth, taking nothing of the Gentiles. We therefore ought to welcome such, that we may be fellow-workers for the truth.

I wrote somewhat unto the church: but Diotrephes, who loveth to have the preeminence among them, receiveth us not. Therefore, if I come, I will bring to remembrance his works which he doeth,[3] prating against us with wicked words; and not content therewith, neither doth he himself receive the brethren, and them that would he forbiddeth and casteth [them] out of the church.[4] Beloved, imitate not that which is evil, but that which is good. He that doeth good is of God: he that doeth evil hath not seen God. Demetrius hath the witness of all [men], and of the truth itself: yea, we also bear witness: and thou knowest that our witness is true.[5]

I had many things to write unto thee, but I am unwilling to write [them] to thee with ink and pen:[6] but I hope shortly to see thee, and we shall speak face to face. Peace [be] unto thee. The friends salute thee. Salute the friends by name.

————••••————

[1] Evidently this is not the same "elder" as in the other letter.
[2] But he is just as glad to communicate with someone who agrees with him.
[3] Diotrephes is junior to the "elder;" Beta here is a persuasion of the young.
[4] Not just refusal of Alpha visitors, but excommunication of Alpha brethren.
[5] For this phrase, see John 21:24, from the last addition to the Gospel of John..
[6] Even in this small detail, 3 John mimics 2 John.

Reflections

Like 2 John, this letter harps on "truth," so it seems that doctrine is hardening on both sides. Everyone thinks they are right; a dangerous situation.

For 3 John, the old system of assisting visitors still exists, or it would if their opponents would permit it. The head of the other church, "Diotrephes," is refusing hospitality to Alpha visitors or travelers, and he excommunicates those who would give it. That is, Diotrephes is doing what the "elder" in 2 John urged *his* correspondent to do: refuse contact with the other side.

Attempts have been made to locate Gaius, the writer's correspondent in the other church. We know of several people with that name (a common Latin one; Julius Caesar also bore it). A Gaius was mentioned by Paul, as one of the few people he baptized in Corinth. Another is said in Acts to be a Macedonian among the traveling companions of Paul; he was involved in a confrontation with Demetrius and the silversmiths in Ephesus. These people might just possibly be still alive at this time, and occupying positions of authority in the churches, just as Onesimus was still flourishing in Ephesus. Perhaps more likely, these letters were made up to dramatize a current conflict, and the writer picked up the names Gaius and Demetrius from Acts, and used them (changing Demetrius to Diotrephes) as the opponents in his composition, with Gaius as the good guy, and Diotrephes as the bad guy. Even as fictions, we may accept them as dramatizing a contemporary issue, just as we cherish Mark's lively creation, the spunky Syrophoenician woman – both tell us about something which, even if fictionally expressed, does represent a historical truth.

The Betas, in real time, had taken over the 1 John Alpha *letter*, and turned it to their purposes. Here we get a picture of the Betas taking over a *church*. Doctrine is hardening, the two will not tolerate each other, excommunication appears. The Apostolic courtesies are no more. The former communication between churches, and accommodation within churches, has broken down.

Excommunication, the device of "Diotrephes," is a lady with many friends, as the Alpha and Beta factions were soon to discover to their cost.

Division

56. Expulsion from the Synagogues
Babylonian Talmud: Berakhot 28b-29a

The increasing insistence of some Jesus followers on the divinity of Jesus, their replacement of God by Jesus at many points, and their reading of the Scriptures as prophecies of Jesus, were increasingly distasteful to those Jews who were not followers of Jesus, and most of all to the Temple leadership. This tension reached a crisis when the Romans destroyed the Temple, depriving Judaism of its sacrificial center. This presented Judaism with an ultimatum: to follow its own universalist trend, or to stay centered on sacrifice. The choice was for sacrifice. In the urgent process of preserving the Temple cult and its associated Sanhedrin court in a diffused form, masterminded by Yohanan, other matters were put on hold.

Some of those "other matters" were taken up when the new arrangement became more stable, and Gamaliel II became the leader at Yabneh, around 80. This passage, from the late but seemingly credible Babylonian Talmud, tells how the daily prayers were expanded by a new addition, intended to deal with the problem of the Jesus sect.[1]

Rabban Gamaliel said to the sages, Is there no one who knows how to compose a Benediction against the minim?[2] Samuel the Less stood up and composed it:

"For the apostates let there be no hope. And let the arrogant government be speedily uprooted in our days. Let the Nozrim[3] and the minim be destroyed in a moment, and let them be blotted out of the Book of Life and not be inscribed together with the righteous. Blessed art thou, O Lord, who humblest the arrogant."

---·••··---

[1]This is a delicate matter, one on which many on both sides are presently in denial. For a careful account, and to me a convincing one, see Martyn **History** 46-66.

[2]A cover term for "heretics;" the word "Christians" never occurs in the Mishnah.

[3]Usually interpreted as "Nazarenes," that is, Christians. But it more likely represents the Nazoreans or followers of John the Baptist, the other Messianic sect. See below.

Reflections

The "arrogant government" is probably not that of occupying Rome, but rather the arrogant Jesus sectarians, who had dared to take the leadership role, in reinterpreting the Scriptures against the traditional understanding.

The Book of Life: the list of those who are to be saved, was a common conception. Paul, writing to Timothy, his associate and "true yokefellow," and asking him to reconcile two feuding women at Philippi, mentions it:

> I entreat Euodia, and I entreat Syntyche, to be of the same mind in the Lord. Yea, I beseech thee also, true yokefellow: Help these women, for they labored with me in the Gospel, with Clement also, and the rest of my fellow-workers, whose names are in the Book of Life. (Philippians 4:2-3)

" Life" here is life eternal, the reward of the righteous.

To pray for the eternal damnation of the sect to which one belonged was not a viable option for any Jesus follower. At the same time, to refuse synagogue prayers was to refuse synagogue fellowship. Those synagogues to which news of this new prayer came, and which adopted it,[4] were no longer open to Jesus followers. But once the Jesus followers left the synagogue and the fellowship of the Jews, they also forfeited the Jewish exemption from Emperor worship, and were liable to the death penalty which was the cost of refusing it.

Who exactly were excluded by this new prayer? It is natural to read Nozrim as "Nazarenes," but then, who were the separately named minim (the heretics)? It seems that the John the Baptist sect (which, with the Jesus followers, was the other major Messianic sect at this period) were called Nazoreans in early times, and their tradition implies that they were expelled from Jerusalem at some point, leading to a search for refuge which ended up in present-day Iran and Iraq, where many Mandaeans still reside. If so, then the plain "minim" may have been the more visible Jesus sect, which unlike the Baptists had been making converts among the Gentiles (yet another source of offense to more traditional Jews). The Jesus people were an irritation in the synagogues, and their success in attracting converts made them a rival of mainstream Judaism.

So here at last the question comes to a head: Who owns Judaism?

We have seen the use of excommunication by the Jesus groups, as a way of removing from their fellowship those whose erroneous thinking was considered to endanger the faith of others. Here, as far as the available evidence suggests, is the largest instance of excommunication in early times.

Its effects were profound.

---

[4]The qualification is important. There is evidence for some mixed synagogues in the following centuries, so acceptance and implementation cannot have been universal. But enough to make a difference which shows up in all the texts of that period.

57. Rejecting Judaism
Acts 28:17-31

A final stage of Luke-Acts, Acts II, was written in response to the showdown with Judaism. The end of Acts II envisions Paul under house arrest in Rome. Paul calls the Jews together; he preaches his message. They refuse it. And Paul declares that henceforth the Christians will seek converts only among Gentiles. As far as Luke is here concerned, Christianity is finished as a Jewish sect.

And it came to pass, that after three days he called together those that were the chief of the Jews: and when they were come together, he said unto them, I, brethren, though I had done nothing against the people, or the customs of our fathers, yet was delivered prisoner from Jerusalem into the hands of the Romans. Who, when they had examined me, desired to set me at liberty, because there was no cause of death in me. But when the Jews spake against it, I was constrained to appeal unto Caesar; not that I had aught whereof to accuse my nation. For this cause therefore did I entreat you to see and to speak with [me]: for because of the hope of Israel I am bound with this chain. And they said unto him, We neither received letters from Judaea concerning thee, nor did any of the brethren come hither and report or speak any harm of thee. But we desire to hear of thee what thou thinkest: for as concerning this sect, it is known to us that everywhere it is spoken against. And when they had appointed him a day, they came to him into his lodging in great number; to whom he expounded [the matter], testifying the kingdom of God, and persuading them concerning Jesus, both from the law of Moses and from the prophets, from morning till evening. And some believed the things which were spoken, and some disbelieved. And when they agreed not among themselves, they departed after that Paul had spoken one word, Well spake the Holy Spirit through Isaiah the prophet unto your fathers, saying, Go thou unto this people, and say, By hearing ye shall hear, and shall in no wise understand; And seeing ye shall see, and shall in no wise perceive: For this people's heart is waxed gross, And their ears are dull of hearing, And their eyes they have closed; Lest, haply they should perceive with their eyes, And hear with their ears, And understand with their heart, And should turn again, And I should heal them.

Be it known therefore unto you, that this salvation of God is sent unto the Gentiles: they will also hear. [And when he had said these words, the Jews departed, having much disputing among themselves]. And he abode two whole years in his own hired dwelling, and received all that went in unto him, preaching the kingdom of God, and teaching the things concerning the Lord Jesus Christ with all boldness, none forbidding him.

Reflections

Luke, to hear him tell it,[1] accompanied Paul from his detention in Caesarea and his shipwreck in Malta, and to Rome, where he was to be tried by Caesar. He thus invites us to accept this last scene as an eyewitness account. It is instead emblematic; the third and last time in Acts when Paul, being refused by the local Jews, turns instead to the Gentiles.[2] Luke is writing in approximately the year 88, and this is his response to the rejection of the Jesus sect by the Jewish leadership, shortly before. He responds by rejecting Judaism.

The terms of the scene are carefully chosen. Luke has avoided copying the denunciation of the crowd by Jesus in Mark's Sermon by the Sea, perhaps due to its excessive harshness, but he uses it here. Given proper space on the page, this Isaiah quote looks like this:

> Go thou unto this people, and say:
> By hearing ye shall hear, and shall in no wise understand.
> And seeing, ye shall see, and shall in no wise perceive.
>
> For this people's heart is waxed gross,
> And their ears are dull of hearing,
> And their eyes they have closed,
>
> Lest haply they should perceive with their eyes
> And hear with their ears,
> And understand with their heart,
>
> And should turn again,
> And I should heal them. (Isaiah 6:9-10)

This is the Isaiah "cursing oracle," and in this somber Roman setting, with nascent Christianity and threatened Judaism facing each other across the room, it is even more ominous.

What had been proclaimed by Gamaliel II in about 85 made its way slowly through the synagogues of the Diaspora. Not all the synagogues adopted it, but those that did make a widening circle, outward from Yabneh. First came Syria, where Luke, who is extending his History of Christianity for just that purpose, puts on record a sort of defiant counter-rejection. We have just read it.

Next in line geographically was Ephesus.

---

[1] Several passages in Acts II are not told in the third person, but in the first: "we." This invites the inference that the author, Luke, was actually a participant in the events he narrates, and was thus himself a companion of Paul. This is probably a subtle fiction; Luke uses it to give his account that much more authority with his readers.

[2] The other two were in Asia, Acts 13:44-47 (an obvious interpolation) and in Achaia, Acts 18:4-6. Note the identical exit line – as it were, three strokes of doom. Luke is fond of using threes to make a point, as we saw in Chapter 37.

58. The Last Farewell
John 16-17

At the end of John 14, as the disciples were leaving the Last Supper, Jesus had said, Come, let us be going, and the narrative continued with him and his disciples in the Garden of Gethsemane, where Jesus was arrested by Temple soldiers led by Judas. Later, the author of John found other things he wanted Jesus to say by way of leavetaking, and another chapter, John 15, was inserted to accommodate them. Still later, as a final leavetaking, John 16, was added (plus a long prayer by Jesus, in John 17). Here is the John 16 leavetaking. It repeats the Paraclete promise from John 15, but with an important difference.

These things have I spoken unto you, that ye should not be caused to stumble. They shall put you out of the synagogues: yea, the hour cometh, that whosoever killeth you shall think that he offereth service unto God. And these things will they do, because they have not known the Father, nor me. But these things have I spoken unto you, that when their hour is come, ye may remember them, how that I told you.

And these things I said not unto you from the beginning, because I was with you. But now I go unto him that sent me; and none of you asketh me, Whither goest thou? But because I have spoken these things unto you, sorrow hath filled your heart. Nevertheless I tell you the truth: It is expedient for you that I go away; for if I go not away, the Paraclete will not come unto you; but if I go, I will send him unto you. And he, when he is come, will convict the world in respect of sin, and of righteousness, and of judgment: of sin, because they believe not on me; of righteousness, because I go to the Father, and ye behold me no more; of judgment, because the prince of this world hath been judged.[1] I have yet many things to say unto you, but ye cannot bear them now. Howbeit when he, the Spirit of truth,[2] is come, he shall guide you into all the truth; for he shall not speak from himself; but what things soever he shall hear, [these] shall he speak; and he shall declare unto you the things that are to come. He shall glorify me; for he shall take of mine, and shall declare [it] unto you . . .

---

[1] Etymologically "Advocate," in many Bibles translated "Comforter." Its meaning changes between one layer of John and the next. In early layers, the Paraclete reminds the disciples of Jesus and interprets his words. In this late layer, the Paraclete sometimes becomes an accuser of the sins of the world. This is a response to the exclusion from the synagogues, which made enemies, not neighbors, of Christians and other Jews.

[2] Here, John 16 continues the earlier meaning of Paraclete: the felt continuity of Christ among his followers, after his death.

Reflections

The Gospel of John was written in Ephesus, and it was in Ephesus that the wave of expulsion persecutions was next felt. The author of John, having already opened up his Gospel to add John 15, *re*opened it to record a prophecy of Jesus about expulsions from synagogues, adding that those who had brought that about felt they were serving God, as in their own way they doubtless were. The beginning of John 16 puts that new prophecy of Jesus into the record.

John 16 goes on to give a different function given to the Paraclete, the Spirit who will be with the disciples, replacing the bodily Jesus, after his death. The Paraclete had had a consoling function (whence the translation "Comforter") and a memory function: to recall what Jesus had said and explain its meaning. Here is how John 15 had put it:

> But when the Paraclete is come, whom I will send unto you from the Father, even the Spirit of Truth, which proceedeth from the Father, he shall bear witness of me, and ye also bear witness, because ye have been with me from the beginning. (John 15:26-27)

To have "been with Jesus from the beginning" was to be able to report what he had done and said. This the Apostles had done; now, the Paraclete has that role: expounding to believers the content and meaning of the faith they already have.

The tone in John 16 is quite different. Just after dealing with the expulsions from the synagogue, "Jesus" goes on to say:

> Nevertheless, I tell you the truth; it is expedient for you that I go away, for if I go not away the Paraclete will not come unto you, but if I go, I will send him unto you. And he, when he is come, will convict the world in respect of sin, and of righteousness, and of judgement; of sin, because they believe not on me; of righteousness, because I go to the Father, and ye behold me no more; of judgement, because the prince of this world hath been judged. (John 16:7-11)

That is, the Paraclete is now a judge of the world, an accuser of wrongdoing, doubtless including the expulsion "prayer" and its perpetrators.

Having thus made Jesus or his proxy a defender in the present, the author then added John 17, a prayer of Jesus which puts the Paraclete *into the future*. After praying for his immediate disciples, Jesus continues:

> Neither for these only do I pray, but for them also that believe on me through their word, that they may all be one, even as thou, Father, art in me and I in thee, that they also may be in us, that the world may believe that thou didst send me. (John 17:20-21)

Luke, speaking through "Paul" (Chapter 56), had turned the church in a new direction, accepting the final break with Judaism. The author of John, speaking through "Jesus," looks ahead – to the final triumph of the unified churches.

Meanwhile, the persecutions themselves would continue to spread.

59. Emergency in Pontus
1 Peter 1:1-2 and 4:12 – 5:14

The crisis had spread to the northern part of Asia. To the baptismal homily of a few years earlier, its author now added new material at both ends, turning it into an Epistle of Peter, and sending it out again, to encourage the Christians in that northern region who were suffering these sudden hardships.

Why Peter? He was long dead, but his name carried authority. The Gospel of Matthew at about this time added a few verses[1] in which Jesus makes Peter the future head of the church. The Gospel of John at about this time added a last chapter, John 21, in which Jesus recognizes Peter as the future leader of the flock. Other texts show an interest in coming to be identified with Paul. As time went on, the claim of any text to speak with authority increasingly rested in its adopting the persona of one or another recognized figure.

Theologically, 1 Peter is Paul territory, not only for its Atonement theology, but also for its mention of Paul's associate Silvanus, and its allusion to the legend that Mark had translated for Peter in Rome.

Peter, an apostle of Jesus Christ, to the elect who are sojourners of the Dispersion in Pontus, Galatia, Cappadocia, Asia, and Bithynia, according to the foreknowledge of God the Father, in sanctification of the Spirit, unto obedience and sprinkling of the blood of Jesus Christ: Grace to you and peace be multiplied . . .

Beloved, think it not strange concerning the fiery trial among you, which cometh upon you to prove you, as though a strange thing happened unto you: but insomuch as ye are partakers of Christ's sufferings, rejoice; that at the revelation of his glory also ye may rejoice with exceeding joy. If ye are reproached for the name of Christ, blessed [are ye]; because the [Spirit] of glory and the Spirit of God resteth upon you. For let none of you suffer as a murderer, or a thief, or an evil-doer, or as a meddler in other men's matters, but if [a man suffer] as a Christian, let him not be ashamed; but let him glorify God in this name. For the time [is come] for judgment to begin at the house of God: and if [it begin] first at us, what [shall be] the end of them that obey not the gospel of God?

> And if the righteous is scarcely saved,
> where shall the ungodly and sinner appear?

Wherefore let them also that suffer according to the will of God commit their souls in well-doing unto a faithful Creator.

---

[1]Matthew 16:18-19, an obvious intrusion into what is on both sides of it.

The elders among you I exhort, who am a fellow-elder, and a witness of the sufferings of Christ, who am also a partaker of the glory that shall be revealed: Tend the flock of God which is among you, exercising the oversight, not of constraint, but willingly, according to [the will of] God; nor yet for filthy lucre, but of a ready mind; neither as lording it over the charge allotted to you, but making yourselves examples to the flock. And when the chief Shepherd shall be manifested, ye shall receive the crown of glory that fadeth not away.

Likewise, ye younger, be subject unto the elder. Yea, all of you gird yourselves with humility, to serve one another: for God resisteth the proud, but giveth grace to the humble. Humble yourselves therefore under the mighty hand of God, that he may exalt you in due time; casting all your anxiety upon him, because he careth for you. Be sober, be watchful: your adversary the devil, as a roaring lion, walketh about, seeking whom he may devour, whom withstand steadfast in your faith, knowing that the same sufferings are accomplished in your brethren who are in the world.

And the God of all grace, who called you unto his eternal glory in Christ, after that ye have suffered a little while, shall himself perfect, establish, strengthen you. To him [be] the dominion for ever and ever. Amen.

By Silvanus, our faithful brother, as I account [him], I have written unto you briefly, exhorting, and testifying that this is the true grace of God. Stand ye fast therein. She that is in Babylon, elect together with [you], saluteth you; and [so doth] Mark my son. Salute one another with a kiss of love.

Peace be unto you all that are in Christ.

Reflections

The idea that suffering is grace, and thus leads to salvation, was to continue, leading to a cult of martyrdom. The author also recommends disdain for wealth and other worldly advantage, and greater conformity with society. There is no inconsistency. The sufferings were caused by a refusal of outside authority and custom, and it was wise to minimize that friction. But if that did not work, to accept the inevitable: not as failure, but as success; indeed, as consummation. The death of Jesus had already been rationalized in a similar way by Mark. Here, that kind of thinking is extended to the community of the faithful.

The churches named make a loop, along which apostles from a center (probably Sinope) might efficiently tour their area of concern. The claim of the letter to derive from Peter may have been meant to imply an origin in Rome. The geography of the letter makes an implicit case for Sinope.

Still to come is a letter that undoubtedly *was* sent from Rome.

60. Troubles at Rome
1 Clement 1:1a

Following the Nero persecution, which effectively ended in 64, the churches of Rome had three leaders: Linus, Anacletus, and Clement. We know their names because they are celebrated in the Canon of the Roman mass. The term of each of them seems to have been about twelve years.[1] As the Jesus movement found its bearings in the post-Apostolic age, the next task was to unify the many local churches. This Clement of Rome attempted, in a letter usually dated to 96. At the moment, we are concerned only with the opening of the letter.

Given the low opinion of Christians held by the Roman public (who had been willing spectators at the deaths inflicted on Christians by Nero, until finally sickened by their increasing cruelty), it is possible that the troubles in Syria and Asia had reached Rome around the year 92, and that at least some Romans had responded to the opportunity it presented by denouncing the Christians among them, as had others before them.[2]

The church of God which sojourns in Rome, to the church of God which sojourns in Corinth, to those who are called and sanctified by the will of God through our Lord Jesus Christ. Grace and peace from God Almighty be multiplied to you through Jesus Christ.

Owing to the sudden and repeated misfortunes and calamities which have befallen us, we consider that our attention has been somewhat delayed in turning to the questions disputed among you, beloved . . .

----—··•··—----

[1] The names (with the variant Anencletus; the Roman Mass has Cletus) are given in Eusebius **History** 3:13-15, with the statement that each reigned for twelve years. The uniform twelve year reigns are intrinsically suspicious. But if Linus became leader at Rome the year after the Neronian persecution (that is, directly after the death of Peter), the three reigns will work out to Linus 65-76, Anacletus 77-88, and Clement 89-100. These fit other available information, and may be accepted as a working model.

[2] For the earlier occasions, see Chapters 57 (for Syria), 58 (Ephesus, southern Asia), and 59 (Pontus, northern Asia). There seems to be no comparable text record for Achaia (Roman Greece). We have now arrived at Rome (Italia).

Reflections

This letter of Clement is an important for the history of late 1st century Christianity. For a while, for some churches, it was part of the New Testament canon (it is included in the 5th century Codex Alexandrinus and a few other manuscripts), but it was later grouped with the writings of the Church Fathers, where it is now to be found.

Clement here is merely getting started, by apologizing for his lateness in writing; a variant of the device we see also in the conclusions of 2 and 3 John.[3] Our present point is the excuse he gives, which implies disturbances of the kind we have seen in Syria, Ephesus, and Pontus, moving progressively westward. The point of this chapter is to suggest how far the expulsion prayer reached, and how serious were its effects, though Clement himself has survived.

So much for Clement's introductory reference to past troubles. His real subject lay elsewhere. The ejection of the Christians from what, until then, had been their home religion, regrettable though it was in a merely personal way, opened up administrative opportunities of the most attractive kind.

[3]See Chapters 54 and 55.

61. The Assertion of Control
1 Clement 5-6

The persecution of Nero in Rome, back in 64, had called forth a new kind of leadership at Rome: first Linus (65-77), then Anacletus (78-89), and third Clement (from 90; martyred under Trajan in 101). The new threat to all of Christendom in the 90s led to a push for a unified leadership. In this letter, Clement bids for that leadership. Of all the great cities (and major churches), Corinth, Ephesus, Antioch, and Alexandria, the nearest was Corinth, and at Corinth, there was the useful precedent of Paul's leadership. Taking up Paul's condemnation of factionalism at Corinth (Chapter 32), Clement begins by attacking diversity of opinion. His theme is that all the troubles of the churches are caused by diversity of opinion; what he calls "jealousy."

Through jealousy and envy, the greatest and most righteous pillars of the Church were persecuted and contended unto death. Let us set before our eyes the good apostles. Peter, who because of unrighteous jealousy suffered not one or two but many trials, and having thus given his testimony went to the glorious place which was his due.[1] Through jealousy and strife Paul showed the way to the prize of endurance; seven times he was in bonds, he was exiled, he was stoned, he was a herald both in the East and in the West, he gained the noble fame of his faith, he taught righteousness to all the world, and when he had reached the limits of the West,[2] he gave his testimony before the rulers, and thus passed from the world and was taken up into the Holy Place – the greatest example of endurance.

To these men with their holy lives was gathered a great multitude of the chosen, who were the victims of jealousy and offered among us the fairest example in their endurance under many indignities and tortures. Through jealousy women were persecuted as Danaids and Dircae,[3] suffering terrible and unholy indignities; they steadfastly finished the course of faith and received a noble reward, weak in the body though they were. Jealousy has estranged wives from husbands, and made of no effect the saying of our father Adam, "This is now bone of my bone and flesh of my flesh." Jealousy and strife have overthrown great cities, and rooted up mighty nations.

———————————

[1]Peter was martyred in Rome in the persecution of Nero, not because of jealousy.

[2]This is the myth that Paul had preached in Spain, the western limit of the known world, and thus in his lifetime had been the universal Apostle.

[3]The persecutions referred to are otherwise unknown. Peter and Paul (both of whom died in Rome) are thus Clement's only examples.

Reflections

Paul's letters, besides chiding particular improprieties, had contained some doctrinal and practical pronouncements. If Clement hopes to become the leader of all the churches, he will need to do the same, or better. He does *much* better. His letter goes on and on, becoming as long as a Gospel, and in it Clement preaches his own gospel: a systematic account of all that is necessary for belief.

Clement runs through it all, with much reliance on the Hebrew Scriptures. Moses, and then Paul, are held up as ideals. The Resurrection is preached, and indeed analyzed, in much detail. Obedience to the local church authorities (the elders, or presbyters) is enjoined. At the end, before the concluding blessings, in Chapter 63, comes this summary assertion of central authority:

> It is therefore right that we should respect so many and so great examples, and bow the neck, and take up the position of obedience, so that ceasing from vain sedition, we may gain without any fault the goal set before us as in truth. For you will give us joy and gladness, if you are obedient to the things which we have written through the Holy Spirit, and root out the wicked passion of your jealousy according to the entreaty for peace and concord which we have made in this letter. And we have sent faithful and prudent men, who have lived among us without blame from youth to old age, and they shall be witnesses between you and us. We have done this that you may know that our whole care has been and is directed to your speedy attainment of peace.

Those envoys are mentioned by name at the very end (Chapter 65):

> Send back quickly to us our messengers Claudius Ephebus and Valerius Vito and Fortunatus, in peace with gladness, in order that they may report the sooner the peace and concord which we pray for and desire, that we also may the more speedily rejoice in your good order.

> The grace of our Lord Jesus Christ be with you and with all, in every place, who have been called by God through him, through whom be to him glory, honor, power, and greatness and eternal dominion, from eternity to eternity. Amen.[4]

In addition to the onset of Heavy Church, emanating from Rome in the west, there were also stirrings in the east. Antioch in Syria was already the center of a parallel centralizing tendency, and when the dust of construction later cleared, there would be two centers of organized Christianity.

Alongside all this organization, the more individualistic Gnostic tendencies which we have seen before[5] began to appear in texts of their own.

---

[4]This and the above translations from Lake.
[5]Chapters 44 and 45.

62. The Inner Quest
Gospel of Thomas 1-12

The probable core of the Gospel of Thomas is its first 12 sayings; the authority figure there is not Thomas, but Jacob, the Lord's Brother. The 12 sayings include bits of the Gospels. Here are the parts of those 12 sayings which are not derived from the Gospels. They show an interesting tendency.

In Gnostic thinking, you are not saved by God's favor, or by your obedience to the Law. No, you are saved by your knowledge. But knowledge of what kind? Knowledge gained how?

1 (§2:1-4). Whoever seeks should not cease seeking until he finds. And when he finds, he will be amazed. And when he is amazed, he will be a king. And once he is a king, he will rest.

§2. Those who seek should not stop seeking until they find. When they find, they will rise. When they rise, they will rule, and when they rule, they will find rest.

§3 . . . You who know yourselves will find this. And when you know yourselves, you will know that you are children of the Father . . .

§4. A man old in days will not hesitate to ask a child seven days old about the place of life, and that man will live . . .

§5. Jesus says, Know what is in front of your face, and what is hidden from you will be revealed to you . . .

§6 . . . Jesus says, Don't lie, and don't do what you hate. . .

§7. Blessed the lion that the man will eat, and the lion becomes man. And cursed the man whom the lion eats, and the man becomes a lion.

§11. Jesus said, . . . The dead are not alive, and the living will not die. While you ate what is dead, you made it something living. When you are in the light, what will you do? When you were one, you became two. But when you are become two, what will you become?

§12. The disciples said to Jesus, We know you are going to leave us. Who will be our leader? Jesus said to them, No matter where you are, you are to go to Jacob the Righteous, for whose sake Heaven and Earth were created.

Reflections

At first glance, these non-Gospel sayings seem to be a miscellaneous lot. Those who know Chinese meditation tradition, the Dàu/Dv́ Jīng 道德經, the Nèı Yè 內業 (Gwǎndž 49), and the Mencius, will see a common thread.

§2. The search ends in "rest." The goal of Chinese meditation is repose (níng 寧, NY 3:9) or tranquility (jìng 靜, NY 5:13).

§3. The search for the higher realm begins with inner self-discovery, and ends with the universe. NY 19:2 萬物備存 "all things [the pleroma] will abide." MC 7A4, 萬物皆備於我矣 "all things are complete in me."

§4. The child still recalls the place from which it came. For the infant as complete in virtue, see DDJ 55 含德之厚，比於赤子 "He who holds virtue in its fulness, I would compare to an infant."

§5. "Understand what is in front of you." Chinese meditation starts with the self, NY 4:1 如在於側 "as though it were right beside you."

§6. "Do not tell lies." The idea of truthfulness as personal integrity or self-similarity (chv́ng 誠) appears in the 03c text Jūng Yūng, and in MC 4A12 誠身有道 "There is a way to make the self integral."

§7. The lower appetites, especially sexual desire (here the "lion"), imperil meditation. Will the lower nature (lion) devour the higher nature (man)?

§11. The soul on earth is subject to such false dichotomies as female and male. For the resolution of opposites into unities, see DDJ 2, 故有無相生，難易相成，長短相較，高下相傾，音聲相和，前後相隨。是以聖人處無爲之事，行不言之教 "Thus Existence and Non-existence give rise to each other, Hard and Easy complete each other, Long and Short define each other, High and Low measure each other, Word and Speech harmonize each other, First and Last follow each other. So the Sage puts himself among Acts of Inaction, practices the Teaching Without Words."

Between §7 and §11 now come Matthew's Wise Fisherman (Mt 13:47-50) and Mark's Sower (Mk 4:3-9), on the same theme of focusing on what is important. But without them, the original Thomas core makes its own kind of sense:

§1. These sayings give the secret Way of Life.
§2. Seek it persistently, and you will find rest.
§3. The secret is within you.
§4. Your primal self remembers it.
§5. Begin with the obvious, and the hidden will be clear to you.
§6. Avoid all doubleness; you must be entirely self-consistent.
§7, 11. Avoid all distractions of sexual desire, or they will consume you.
§12. [Recommendation of the text patron, Jacob]

The divine origin of man is hidden, but it may be rediscovered. Jesus in the Philippi Hymn had a divine origin, which he relinquished to descend to earth. His Resurrection inspired many to hope to imitate him in ascending to Heaven. This Teaching of Jacob the Brother tells them – or reminds the adepts who already know – how that is done. *This* is what the Gnostic knows.

63. A Hymn at Daybreak
Odes of Solomon 15

These 42 Odes were written in Syria, and in the local language, Syriac.
They share features with the writings of Ignatius of Antioch (martyred c115),
and belong to the early 2nd century: later than the Thomas core. They know all
the Gospels, not just John (whence the themes of Light and Life), but the others
too (they give space to the Virgin Birth). They show one variety of Christianity
as, so to speak, brushed by the Gnostic tendency within Christianity.

This Ode celebrates the dawn of understanding (Gnosis) in the believer.[1]

As the sun is my joy, to them who seek its daybreak,
so is my joy to the Lord,

Because he is my Sun, and his rays have lifted me up,
and his Light has dismissed all darkness from my face.

Eyes I have obtained in him,
and have seen his holy day;

Ears I have acquired,
and have heard his truth;

The thoughts of knowledge I have acquired,
and have lived fully through him.

I repudiated the way of error,
and went toward him and received salvation from him abundantly,

And according to his generosity he gave to me,
and according to his excellent beauty he made me;

I put on incorruption through his name,
and took off corruption by his grace.

Death has been destroyed before my face,
and Sheol[2] has been vanquished by my word,

And eternal Life has arisen in the Lord's hand,
and it has been declared by his faithful ones,

And have been given without limit to all that trust in him.
Hallelujah![3]

---

[1]Translation from Charlesworth.
[2]Also Gehenna; alternate names for the abode of the damned.
[3]Hebrew for "Praise Jehovah." All these Odes end with this group response.

Reflections

The benefits here received from God are understanding of truth, and also "grace," which need not refer to the Atonement interpretation of Jesus, and can be read as the forgiveness which God extends to the repentant sinner. The "repudiation of error" is then the individual's repentance, which might be interpreted in Alpha terms: a determination to live by what is righteous. Other Odes unmistakably assume the Atonement theology, but this one shows us that the Atonement theology did not blot out its precursor, Repentance theology. Rather, the two existed together in a psychologically workable balance.

The Ephesians hymn quoted in Chapter 49 shows that same balance. Paul himself, always the fighter, was ever ready to wage war for the Atonement, but his successors, though most of them did not lose sight of the idea, distinctly back-burnered it. By this time, and in this place, these once hostile doctrines have reached a situation of conventional acquaintance and mutual repose.

There is a serenity to these Odes, as though far removed from the trifling tribulations of this world, and already taking part in the distant Life to Come. This sense of immediacy, rather than a hope of salvation at some future date, is one characteristic of the Gamma tradition. The immediacy of Gnosticism is part of its universality, and thus part of its appeal, down to the present day.

64. Finding Rest
Odes of Solomon 38:1-5

The Odes are very Jesus-centered. At intervals, the singer extends his arms to invoke the Cross. Christ speaks directly in several Odes. The perilous return of the soul to the high place whence it came, challenged on the way by astral Principalities and Powers, is absent here, as elsewhere in Thomas Christianity, which stands somewhat apart from the Gnostic mainstream.

But at one place, the beginning of Ode 38, we find a seeming reminiscence of the difficult journey of the soul, and the rest which it seeks (as in Thomas 1) at the end of the journey.

I went up into the light of Truth as into a chariot,
and the Truth led me, and caused me to come.

And caused me to pass over chasms and gulfs,
and saved me from cliffs and valleys.

And became for me a haven of salvation,
and set me on the place of immortal Life.

And He went with me and caused me to rest, and did not allow me to err,
because He was and is the Truth.

And there was no danger for me because I constantly walked with Him,
and I did not err in anything because I obeyed Him . . .

Reflections

The element of "rest" is conspicuous in the Odes. Indeed, Ode 26 speaks as though the whole collection was on that theme:

> I poured out praise to the Lord,
> because I am his own.
> And I will recite His holy Ode,
> because my heart is with Him.
> For His harp is in my hand,
> and the Odes of His rest shall not be silent . . .
>
> Who can write the Odes of the Lord,
> or who can read them?
> Or who can train himself for life,
> that he may be saved? . . .

It has therefore been suggested that these 42 Odes were originally designated "The Odes of His Rest." However that may be, the theme of rest is pervasive (it occurs more than 18 times in the 42 Odes), and forms a link between them and Thomas Christianity.

The serenity of the Odes, which derives from their confidence in Christ, should not be taken as evidence that the times themselves were peaceful.

On the contrary.

65. Once More in Pontus
Pliny Letter 96

The troubles of the Nineties continued to recur in the following decades.

In 109, Pliny the Younger was given charge of the north Asian province of Bithynia-Pontus by Emperor Trajan. He worked his way through the territory, cleaning up fiscal irregularities. After two years, he had reached Amisus, the easternmost city of the province. At Sinope, on the Black Sea shore, he was asked to judge cases of Christians who had refused to worship the Emperor, and were subject to the death penalty. Anonymous denunciations poured in. Pliny had never handled such cases, and wrote to Trajan for advice. Pliny's letter includes the only known description of the practice of a Christian church. Here it is.

It is my custom, Sir, to bring before you everything about which I am in doubt. For who can better guide my uncertainty or inform my ignorance? I have never been present at trials of Christians; for that reason, I do not know what the charge usually is and to what extent it is usually punished. I have been in no little uncertainty about whether a distinction should be made between different ages, or whether, however young they may be, they should be treated no differently from the more mature ones; whether pardon should be granted for repentance or whether it is of no help to the man who has been a Christian to have given it up; whether it is the name itself, if it is free from crimes, or the crimes associated with the name which are being punished.

Meanwhile, in the case of those who were prosecuted before me on the charge of being Christians, I followed this procedure. I asked the people themselves whether they were Christians. Those who admitted that they were, I asked a second and a third time, warning them of the punishment. Those who persisted I ordered to be executed. For I was in no doubt that, whatever it might be that they were admitting to, their stubbornness and unyielding obstinacy certainly ought to be punished. There were others of a similar madness whom I have listed as due to be sent on to the city, because they were Roman citizens.

Subsequently, in the course of dealing with the matter, as usually happens, the charge spread widely and more forms of it turned up. An anonymous pamphlet containing the names of many persons was posted. Those who denied that they were or had been Christians, after they had called upon the gods when I dictated the formula, and after they had made offerings of incense and wine to your statue which I had ordered to be brought in with the images of the gods for this purpose, and had also cursed Christ, none of which acts, it is said, those who are truly Christians can be compelled to perform, I decided should be discharged.

Others, named by an informer, said that they were Christians and then denied it; they said that they had in fact been Christians but had given it up, some three years before, some longer ago than that, and a few as much as twenty (non nemo etiam ante viginti). All these also both paid homage to your statue and to the images of the gods and cursed Christ. Moreover, they maintained that this had been the sum of their guilt or error, that they had been in the habit of gathering together before dawn on a fixed day, and of singing antiphonally a hymn to Christ as if to a god, and of binding themselves by oath not to some wickedness but not to commit acts of theft or robbery or adultery, not to break faith, and not to refuse to return money placed in their keeping when called upon to do so. When these ceremonies had been completed, they said it had been their custom to disperse and to meet again to take food, but food that was ordinary and harmless; they said that they had given up doing even this after my edict in which, in accordance with your instructions, I banned secret societies.

So I believed it to be all the more necessary to ascertain what the truth was from two slave women who were called deaconesses[1] and under torture. I found nothing other than a depraved and extravagant superstition.

And so I postponed the hearing and hastened to consult you. For the matter seemed to me worthy of your consideration, especially on account of the number who are endangered. For many persons of every age, of every rank, of both sexes, are and will be brought into danger. The infection of this superstition has spread, not only through the towns, but also through the villages and the countryside; it seems possible for it to be checked and put right. At any rate, it is established that temples which just now were almost abandoned have begun to be thronged, and customary rites which had long been suspended to be renewed, and the flesh of sacrificial victims, for which until recently very few buyers were to be found, to be sold far and wide. From this it is easy to conjecture what a host of people could be reformed, if room were given for repentance.[2]

———••••———

[1] The original Latin is: ex duabus ancillis, quae ministrae dicebantur. It is these reports of later persecutions that enable the dating of the earliest persecutions to about 20 years earlier; see Chapters 56 and following

[2] Translation from Radice.

Reflections

The requirement of Emperor worship was universal in the Empire; only the Jews had been granted an exemption. Once the Jesus sect members had been expelled from the synagogues, they were no longer legally regarded as Jews, and the requirement applied. Once they had had to curse Christ to remain in the synagogues; now they had to curse Christ to stay alive *outside* the synagogues. How many died, over the years, we do not know, but Pliny mentions the cases of at least the two deaconesses, and refers to repeated denunciations and trials going back as much as 20 years. Readers may make their own estimate.

The deaconesses were evidently the leading figures in at least two of these churches. This is a throwback, a pattern persisting despite the post-Apostolic tendency to conform to contemporary society by limiting the role of women. Here, in remote northern Pontus, we see the older way still in being.

These churches were of an older type in another way also: they emphasized the rule against fraud (withholding money owed), which was Jesus' addition to his Five Mosaic Commandments. We have seen that many Alpha documents mention it. By that test, these were Alpha churches.

These churches were most likely founded in the grassroots expansion which began in the lifetime of Jesus. That first wave took the Jesus message south to Alexandria, whence came the Alpha Christian Apollos; north to Pontus; and west to Corinth, where (as Paul later complained) Alpha folk were present.

And the Alpha persuasion, despite lacking an organized institutional base, continued to survive in the years to come.

66. In Later Times
Arius of Alexandria

The human Jesus of Mark was followed by the divinely begotten Jesus of Matthew and Luke, and he in turn by the Johannine Jesus: the God Jesus, who had existed since the beginning of time. Nor was this the ultimate development. By the 4th Century, the doctrine of the Trinity asserted that God, Jesus, and the Holy Spirit were *of one substance*,[1] and indistinguishable. One churchman who held back from this last step, and argued that since the Father had begotten the Son, there must logically have been a time before the Son existed, was Arius of Alexandria (256-336). Even this qualification aroused violent opposition. Wrote Arius to his ally Eusebius of Nicomedia,[2]

> To that most beloved man of God, the faithful and orthodox Eusebius, from Arius, unjustly persecuted by father Alexander because of the all-conquering truth which you, Eusebius, are also defending. . . because the Bishop [Alexander] is severely ravaging and persecuting us and moving against us with every evil. Thus he drives us out of every city like godless men, since we will not agree with his public statement that there was "always a God, always a Son."

-------------····--------------

[1]The Greek term is "homoousia."

[2]Not the famous church historian; that was Eusebius of Caesarea (c260-339). Nicomedia, a natural communication center, was the chief city of Bithynia in Asia Minor. It became the eastern capital of the Roman Empire (under Diocletian, in 286) until Constantine moved it to Byzantium (in 330), which he renamed Constantinople.

Reflections

The matter of Arius came to a head at the Council of Nicea (325), called by Emperor Constantine. The Trinitarian view prevailed. Arius was declared a heretic. His works were burned. Later Emperors were more favorable, but Arius was condemned again at the Second Council of Nicea (381). His ideas survived only among Goths and Vandals, to whom Arius' friend Eusebius of Nicomedia had sent the Gothic convert Ulfilas.

But the lands of these Goths were no small thing. They reached from the Black Sea all the way to the Baltic.

From this area of Central Europe, opposition to the Trinity doctrine emerged again at the time of the Reformation. The targets of the Reformers were many. One was the sale of indulgences, which was protested by Martin Luther's Ninety-Five Theses of 1517. Another was infant baptism, opposed by the Anabaptists, one early statement being the Schleitheim Confession of 1527, written by the Swiss Brethren, distant ancestors of the modern Mennonites. Others sought to restore the uniqueness of God by abandoning the Trinity doctrine. It was denounced by Peter Gonesius at a 1556 meeting of Polish Protestants, leading to the formation of a Polish Brethren church in 1565. The Brethren were joined by the Italian exile Fausto Sozzini (after whom the "Socinian" heresy is named) in 1579, and by the German Johannes Crellius. They had an Academy and an Arian printing house at Racov (1602-1638). Their Latin publications spread their ideas to the rest of Europe.

The Polish Brethren church was dissolved, and the Brethren exiled, in 1658, only to take root in Prussia (where Christopher Crell founded new churches); in Transylvania, at the Unitarian College in Cluj; in the Netherlands, where "Unitarian" treatises of the Brethren were published (and read in France by Voltaire and Pierre Bayle); and in England, where John Biddle republished the Racovian Catechism and other works. Samuel Przypkowski on tolerance and Andrzej Wiszowaty on "rational religion" preceded the work of John Locke.

Many of these ripples of theological opinion were part of the tide of the new science, which drew attention to the idea of God in nature. Isaac Newton knew Samuel Crell, the son of Johannes Crellius. Newton was well informed about events in Poland, and owned books from the Racovian Academy.

English Unitarian ideas were carried to other shores when Joseph Priestley founded a church in Philadelphia, sometimes attended by Thomas Jefferson. Thus did the Alpha strand of Christian theology emerge in the modern world.

But religion is more than theology; it is also what you *do*. And throughout all this history, down to yesterday, every Christian mother who told her child to do good and not evil became, for that moment, an *Alpha* Christian mother.

This is the deep continuity, the true permanence, of ancient Alpha.

Afterword

That's the end of the book. That is what happened, as near as I can tell. There remains the question, What does this mean for us today?

Modern Americans read of the Pilgrim settlers, and find them affecting. They visit their settlements, look inside their houses, sit in their chairs. But they do not go home and imitate the Pilgrims' towns, their furniture, or their ideas. Perhaps that is a useful model for modern Christians visiting the Christian past.

Far back in the Hebrew scriptures, there appeared the idea that what God wants of people here below is not the blood of animal sacrifices, but decent treatment of our human neighbors; that priestly purity was not the last word in religious duty, but only the first. Jesus, though he still looked for victory in war as the reward of the repentance of Israel, took that one step further. The Gentile converts who came into the Jesus sect, at first unbidden and even resented, showed how far beyond national Israel that ethical insight might apply. And so Christianity became not one more Jewish sect, but a world religion, though one still dragging along with it some theological baggage from its Jerusalem period. Perhaps that is unfinished business, as the old inspiration continues to operate.

In an essay on "Contemporary Jewish Religion" contributed to Peake's Commentary (1920), Claude G Montefiore observed,

> The religious effects of the combination of monotheism with nationalism were deeply marked both for good and evil, for strength and weakness. It certainly promoted an intensity of religious feeling, which, at that time, may not have been attainable in any other way. If the national God had become the One and Only God by being supposed to show an absolute equality of interest in all the nations of the world, it might well have been that this equal interest would have been thought to be a puny interest.
>
> A God who, without mediation or mediator, is equally near to, interested in, and approachable by, the entire human race, a Theism which should be both philosophic and intimate, both pure and warm – for this the Jews have become capable only by slow process of time.

We today are not the end of history. Future ages, if they think of us at all, will find us just as quaint as we now find our cultural ancestors. Perhaps, then, that impetus from an important idea of the early centuries still has a place to go, a way in which it can be more completely realized.

> *What doth Jehovah require of thee, but to do justly, and to love kindness, and to walk humbly with thy God?*

Not to end with a question, or anything, but I think I will leave it at that.

Thanks to readers, for reading. And may something or other in the reading prove to be of use to you hereafter.

End Matter

Chronology

Duplicated from *Alpha* volume 1; see those studies for arguments in detail.
Many dates circa. **Emperors**. *Texts*. *Interpolated passages

28 [**Tiberius**]. John the Baptist preaches at the Jordan; baptism of Jesus
29 John the Baptist executed. Jesus teaches in Galilee; arouses opposition
30 Crucifixion of Jesus. *Mark* begun. Saul of Tarsus persecutes Jesus converts
31 Jacob of Alphaeus replaces Levi at Capernaum
32 Shift to Jerusalem; Matthew replaces Levi at Jerusalem. Resurrection doctrine
33 Conversion of Saul > Paul; he visits Jerusalem to confer with Cephas [Peter]
34 Paul preaches under the direction of Antioch
35
36
37 **Caligula**.
38
39 *Didache* core?
40 Caligula threat to desecrate the Temple is reflected at Mk 13:14
41 Caligula assassinated; desecration threat vanishes. **Claudius**
42 Abandonment of prediction of Signs of the End (Mk 13:32-37)
43 Atonement doctrine appears; is added to *Mark* (Mk 10:45, 11:24)
44 Paul visits Jerusalem; receives liberal ruling on Gentiles. Herod kills Jacob Zebedee
    Peter flees; Matthew is briefly in charge at Jerusalem
45 *Mark* completed by adjustments for Gentiles. John Mark leaves for Antioch
    Jacob the Lord's Brother succeeds Matthew; counters previous ruling. *Didache* 6:3?
46 Confrontation of Peter and Paul over Gentile commensality at Antioch
    John Mark accompanies Paul; is unsuccessful in preaching to Gentiles at Perga
47 John Mark goes to Alexandria, where he becomes a leading figure
48
49
50
51 *1 Thessalonians*
52
53 *Philippians* conflation includes a letter from Paul's imprisonment at Ephesus
    Galatians. *Philemon*. Onesimus becomes Paul's manager at Ephesus
54 **Nero**
55 *Didache* 12:2-14:3, authorizing longer Apostolic visits such as those of Paul?
56 *1 and 2 Corinthians*. Paul proposes a second collection for Jerusalem
    Factions at Corinth: Paul, Apollos, Cephas [Peter], "Christ" [Alpha Christians]
57 *Romans*. Faith/works dispute between Paul and *Jacob* [of Alphaeus]
58 Paul delivers collection to Jerusalem; is arrested there and detained at Caesarea
59 Paul transported to Rome
60 Paul executed at Rome
61 *Didache* 1-5 (Two Ways tract) added?
62 Jacob the Lord's Brother killed by Jewish authorities at Jerusalem
63
64 Nero persecutions at Rome. Peter killed. Post-Apostolic period begins
65 Linus becomes first post-Apostolic leader at Rome
66 *Luke A* written to fill post-Apostolic gap in Christian literature. Jewish War begins
67 Josephus surrenders to Vespasian at Jerusalem
68 **Galba**. *Matthew* written as conservative counter to *Luke A*

69	**Otho. Vitellius. Vespasian.**
70	Jerusalem Temple destroyed by Titus
	Rabbinic center established by Yohanan ben Zakkai at Yabneh (Jamnia) in Judaea
71	Paul's letters edited by Onesimus, Timothy, Titus, Silvanus, Sosthenes
	Paul's editors know *Luke A* and *Matthew*
	Colossians written as preface to the Pauline collection. Collection published
72	*Luke B* written to counter *Matthew*. Lk 21:20 updates Mk 13:14
	Acts I (Ac 1:1-15:34) knows Paul's letters. Equates Peter and Paul; stresses amity
	Post-70 detail added at Mt 22:7 to imitate *Luke B*'s post-70 update at Lk 21:20
73	Jewish War ends
74	
75	Josephus *Jewish War* (lost Aramaic original)
76	Did 15:1-3 (on local church governance) added?
77	Anacletus becomes second leader at Rome
78	
79	**Titus.**
	Josephus *Jewish War*, Greek translation (Books 1-6)
80	Gamaliel II becomes leader at Yabneh. *1 Peter A*, a baptismal homily
81	**Domitian.** Onesimus becomes Bishop at Ephesus. *Ephesians*
82	*Didache* 16 (Matthean-style Apocalypse) added?
83	
84	
85	Birkat ha-Minim composed at Yabneh.
86	Birkat effect in Judaea; no literary reflection
87	Birkat effect in Syria
88	*Acts II* (Antioch) responds to Birkat separation by "turning to the Gentiles"
89	Birkat effect in Iconium; no literary reflection
	Clement becomes third leader at Rome
90	*John D* (*9:2, *12:42, 16:2; Ephesus) speaks of exclusion from synagogues
91	Birkat effect in Pontus and Nicomedia
	1 Peter B (1:1-2, 4:12–5:14) reflects the Birkat crisis in Pontus
	1 Peter B, with added Petrine personalia, bids for recognition as Petrine
	Matthew, with added *16:18-20, bids for recognition as Petrine
92	*John E*, with added *Jn 21, bids for recognition as Petrine
93	*Hebrews*, with added Pauline personalia *13:22-25, bids for recognition as Pauline
	Josephus *Antiquities*, apologetic defense of Judaism as a philosophy
94	Birkat effect in Rome; later recalled by Clement in *1 Clement*
95	
96	**Nerva.** *1 Clement* moves to assert domination of other churches by Rome
	1 Clement begins by recalling the previous (c94) Birkat crisis in Rome
97	
98	**Trajan.**
99	
100	Death of Clement, said to have been martyred under Trajan
105	
106	
107	
108	Renewed trials of denounced Christians at Pontus
109	
110	Statement of Papias about *Mark* and *Matthew*, quoted by Eusebius
111	Pliny, after consulting with Trajan, executes unrepentant Christians at Pontus

Works Cited

Here are details for the books or articles mentioned in this book, plus some findings which this book has accepted as part of its understanding of the texts.

.

Alpha. *The Project's reader-friendly journal for Early Christianity.*

Ante-Nicene Christian Library. v3 1867; repr Elibron 2005

Aziz S Atiya. History of Eastern Christianity. Gorgias 2010

Walter Bauer. Orthodoxy and Heresy in Earliest Christianity. 1934; Fortress 1971

Frank W Beare. The Sequence of Events in Acts 9-15 and the Career of Peter.
JBL v62 (1943) 294-306. *Solves the problem of "Jacob" at Jerusalem.*

Frank W Beare. 1 Peter. 3ed Oxford 1997. *Recognizes a two-layer structure.*

E Bruce Brooks. Acts-Luke. Alpha v1 (2017) 147-161. *Strata in Luke and Acts.*

E Bruce Brooks. Alexandrian Motifs in Chinese Texts.
Sino-Platonic Papers #96 (1999)

E Bruce Brooks. Four Gospel Trajectories. Alpha v1 (2017) 27-28

E Bruce Brooks. Luke's Parable of the Canny Steward. Alpha v1 (2017) 162-170.

E Bruce Brooks. Luke's Sermon on the Way. Alpha v1 (2017) 171-183

E Bruce Brooks. Mark at Perga. Alpha v1 (2017) 96-103

E Bruce Brooks. The Reader in the Text. Alpha v1 (2017) 12-16
Many interpolations in the Gospels belong to this widespread type.

E Bruce Brooks. The Resurrection of Jesus in Mark. Alpha v1 (2017) 80-87

E Bruce Brooks. Thomas A. Alpha v1 (2017) 206-208. *The meditation tradition,*

E Bruce Brooks. The Two Ways. Alpha v1 (2017) 39-47

E Bruce Brooks. Yoḥanan ben Zakkai. Alpha v1 (2017) 201-208

E Bruce Brooks and A Taeko Brooks. The Original Analects. Columbia 1998

E Bruce Brooks and A Taeko Brooks. The Emergence of China.
Warring States Project 2015

James Hamilton Charlesworth. The Odes of Solomon. Oxford 1973

Raymond F Collins. Letters that Paul Did Not Write. Michael Glazier 1980

Herbert Danby. The Mishnah. Oxford 1933; repr Hendrickson 2015

April D DeConick. The Original Gospel of Thomas in Translation.
T & T Clark 2007

Burton Scott Easton. The Pastoral Epistles. Scribner 1947

J K Elliott. The Apocryphal New Testament. Oxford 1993

Morton S Enslin. "Luke" and Paul. JAOS v58 (1931) 81-91
The first to realize that Luke knew Paul's letters.

Eusebius. Ecclesiastical History. [Loeb] Harvard 1926, 1932

Mark R Fairchild. Why Perga? BAR v39 #6 (2013) 52-59, 84

Joseph A Fitzmyer. Luke. 2v Doubleday 1970, 1982.
Argues (at 1/304-312) that the Birth Narrative is secondary in Luke.

Robert M Grant. Gnosticism: A Source Book of Heretical Writings. Harper 1961

Robert H Gundry. Matthew. Eerdmans 1982. *Argues for a pre-70 date.*

Adolph Harnack. Luke the Physician. 1906; Williams & Norgate 1909

David Hawkes. Ch'u Tz'u. Oxford 1959
   Includes two poems on summoning the soul.

Harris Hirschberg. Simon Bariona and the Ebionites. JBL v51 (1942) 171-191

A M Hunter. Paul and His Predecessors. 2ed SCM 1961
   Includes (at 39-44) Lohmeyer's analysis of the Philippi Hymn.

Joseph Klausner. Jesus of Nazareth. Macmillan 1926

Kirsopp Lake. Apostolic Fathers I [Loeb]. Harvard 1912

J Louis Martyn. History and Theology in the Fourth Gospel. 1968; 3ed Knox 2003
   Careful and convincing account of the effect of the Birkat ha-Minim.

Alec McCowen. St Mark's Gospel [1990 performance, 105 minutes].
   Daystar [DVD]

Max McLean. Mark's Gospel [performance, 101 minutes]. Vision [DVD]

Eduard Meyer. Ursprung und Änfänge des Christentums. 2v Cotta 1921-1923
   The first to discern that all references to the Twelve are exiguous in Mark.

C G Montefiore. The Synoptic Gospels. 2ed Macmillan 1927

Jacob Neusner. The Mishnah. Yale 1988

Jacob Neusner. The Tosefta. 2v Hendrickson 2002

Elaine Pagels. The Gnostic Paul. Trinity 1975

Ben Edwin Perry. Babrius and Phaedrus. [Loeb] Harvard 1965

Betty Radice. Letters of the Younger Pliny. Penguin 1969

Hermann von Soden. Die wichtigsten Fragen im Leben Jesu. Duncker 1904
   The first attempt to divide Mark into strata.

Vincent Taylor. The Gospel According to St Mark. Macmillan 1952
   The first to recognize the stratified nature of the predictions in Mark 13.

Charles Cutler Torrey. Documents of the Primitive Church. Harper 1941

William Varner. The Didache. University Press of America 2007

Philipp Vielhauer. On the "Paulinism" of Acts; in Keck ed, Studies in Luke-Acts
   (Abingdon 1966) 33-50. *First detected the absence of the Atonement in Acts.*

Urban C von Wahlde. The Gospel and Letters of John. 3v Eerdmans 2010
   A three-layer stratification model for the Gospel of John.

William O Walker Jr. Interpolations in the Pauline Letters. Sheffield 2001

William O Walker Jr. Paul and His Legacy. Polebridge 2015
   These two collections are the Bible of the subject for the serious student.

Adela Yarbro Collins. Mark. Fortress 2007
   Recognizes that the earliest Passion Narrative lacked the Empty Tomb.

Passages Included

Texts are listed alphabetically within sections. References are to pages.

Subject Index

Pages are numbered from the very beginning; thus the Preface is on pages 7-8.